There's a lamb climbing

I suppose a lamb climbing out of the oven isn't major problem for most households, and indeed it isn't a problem for us either to be honest. I'd even see it as a sign of success.

Our Rayburn, like others of its kind, has a hot chamber below the oven. This is a useful facility, but especially at lambing time. The relative sizes of the oven and the lamb are such that a lamb placed on a flattened 750gm Kellogg's Cornflake packet will just nicely slide into the hot chamber. At this point you may be asking why? The answer is relatively simple. At lambing time, nature pretty well takes its course. A ewe will have one, ideally two, occasionally three, or far more rarely, four lambs. With singles, she's normally on top of her game and they tend to be a biggish lamb anyway so there aren't too many problems. Once you get to twins and triplets you can find that one or more of the lambs might be neglected or a bit slow.

So as soon as possible after they're born, the lambs are checked out. Put a bit of iodine on the navel to stop infection creeping in and make sure they've got a feed of colostrum inside them.

Some lambs can just be a bit wet and cold; when you're that size and born outside, exposure is a indisputable risk. For them there is a plastic tub with some straw bedding, placed under a lamp. This will warm them up nicely, and some might spend a day or more in there before they're strong enough to unite with a hopefully doting mother.

For some, more drastic measures are called for. We've put lambs in warm water before now, (not too warm, about 105F is supposed to be the top temperature) just to warm them up in a hurry.

Finally for others, there's the Rayburn. It tends to be first thing in the morning when the Rayburn isn't 'turned up'. So it is very pleasantly warm rather than getting ready to cook something.

Occasionally you have to take special measures. I remember one measure my father used when I was about eight or nine. When my parents were married back in the 1950s, amongst their wedding presents was a bottle of whisky, a bottle of rum and a bottle of gin. Well the gin went to make sloe gin. In Cumbria rum isn't merely a drink, it is a major culinary ingredient. The rum bottle would disappear into rum butter and rum sauce in the first couple of years of their married life. But the whisky just sat there, unopened and unheeded.

Until after breakfast one morning, the lamb in the oven wasn't responding. So my father opened the whisky bottle, put a tiny drop of whisky onto an apostle spoon and used that to pour the whisky into the lamb's mouth in a last desperate attempt to save the little mite.

It shivered a bit, coughed and died.

A couple of years later, an aunt of mine trapped her hand in a car door, and my mother hurried her into our kitchen, sat her down, and sent me to get the bottle of whisky (unused since the lamb incident.)

I brought it and my mum poured her sister some in a glass with some water. As my aunt drank it, I watched, with the callous intent of an eight year old, to see if she coughed and died as well.

So back to our lamb, lying on its cornflake packet; if it sits up, that's good. If it manages to somehow wiggle out and end up on the kitchen floor, that is also good (no matter what Jess, our elderly and three-legged Border Collie thinks). But the best sign of all is when, once on the floor, it stands up and totters off under its own steam to find somewhere more interesting.

Note. Before welcoming these ovine perambulations it's as well to remember that the lamb is not in anyway toilet trained and one should not encourage it to venture into areas that might be carpeted.

Just getting by

Have you noticed how, when people portray poverty in fantasy, they dwell on the squalor, and somehow even the squalor is more squalid in fantasy worlds. The cess pits are deeper, the chife is more intense and the degradation more complete.
 Yet a few days ago I was taking apart a building. I have to get this job done because only the woodworm are holding it together and they appear to be losing interest. Anyway at one point I was looking down on the roof trusses from above. Now the piece of timber that stretches across the building, the bottom of the truss, is sometimes called 'the cord'. They form a handy storage area, long pieces of timber can be stuck up there out of the way, and then you can stick all sorts of rubbish on top of them.
So now I was looking down at all the stuff that had been stuck there, and what riches did I find?
Well there were some plastic bags, bundled together, 'because they always come in'. Those I put there. But there was a cart shaft. Back in 1958 or thereabouts my grandfather had obviously decided that the tractor was here to stay. Now cart shafts bolt into the side of the cart, and what they'd done was just unbolted the shafts and H Armer and Son, our local agricultural engineer, had made a steel drawbar which bolted back onto the same place. I even remember the cart the shafts came from. I rode on it many times as a kid.
But with the new drawbar in place, my dad and my grandfather had put the shafts up carefully out of the way, 'in case they come in.'
Next to them was a battered model shippon. Not sure if anyone can remember back into the late 1950s but timber wasn't good to come by. It might not have been formally on ration, but I can remember my father squirreling away anything that looked at all decent. Anyway at some point around then he'd made me a model farm and I was looking down at the last surviving bits.

Can you remember the old tea chests? Well he'd obviously got a couple of the old tea chests and he'd taken them apart and cut them up somehow and used them to make the farm buildings. When I saw the buildings I also remembered the cows. He'd cut out the silhouette of a cow in wood, quite a lot of them if memory serves, and my mother had taken them to the school where she taught and painted them. Other kids might have had more three-dimensional cows, but mine were most definitely the right colour and markings.

Looking back at the world I knew then, in reality fantasy writers have got it wrong. Well most of them have, there is one honourable exception and that is Terry Pratchett. I'm going from memory here, I think it is in 'Guards Guards', but certainly it is an observation Captain Vimes makes to himself. The smell of poverty is the smell of soap. You didn't have money so you tried harder. What you'd got might not be special but it was clean and it was looked after.

We're not talking the poverty of the maxed out credit card or of debt. We're talking of the poverty of people who were far too wise, and probably far too proud, to borrow in the first place. But most importantly, these people didn't even think of themselves as poor. They knew what 'poor' meant; they put money in the collection plate for people abroad they knew were poor. If you asked they were getting by. Not comfortable, but getting by.

The horns of elfland, faintly blowing.

I was minding my own business. Honest. I was there with a chainsaw cleaning up an old hedge. It's one of those jobs that my grandfather really should have got round to, and my dad never had time to do. So we have a hedge which consists of clumps of Sycamore. They come up from a common bole and some of them are trees in their own right; they're over a foot across.

So I come along with the chainsaw and cut them off so young growth can come up and we get back the hedge my grandfather knew. Some of them grow out over the sunken lane. These I drop off into the lane, they're beyond saving, and will be next winter's firewood. If I don't there's the danger that if we get a good westerly gale when they've got leaves on, they'll fall over, tearing their roots out. Still I leave one nice standard per set of roots, and all the smaller stuff. With the big stuff gone, I'll come back and lay the lesser stuff so that it'll make some pretence of being a hedge. In twenty years it'll be a good 'un.
Anyway there I was, when I heard the sound of bagpipes. I stopped the chainsaw and listened again. I caught it again. I looked round, someone with an unusual ring-tone? There was no sign of anyone. Something on a car or tractor radio? Again there was one tractor working and it doesn't have a functioning radio. Anyway the pipes stopped.
So I carried on, and as I dropped the next big sycamore I could hear over the chainsaw vague hints that the pipes had started again. I stopped the saw and put it down. There were the bagpipes again. By this time I came to the conclusion they were coming from the direction of the main road, near the church. That would put them just over half a mile away. 'Leccy Board' have one of their transformer boxes there. Was someone working on that and leaving the van radio on perhaps?
Let us get this in perspective here, we're ninety miles south of Carlisle. Pipers are only slightly more common than unicorns. I think that I can say with absolute confidence, I have never stood on any of our hedges and heard the bagpipes before.
At about this time the chainsaw ran out of juice, and the chain needed tightening. So I collected old Jess who'd been watching the whole performance with the analytical eye of an elderly border collie. Now, the pipes had stopped and other than a bit of traffic on the main road, it was quiet. I got home- time for a bit of dinner.
My lady wife arrives back; she'd opened up the church for a burial in our church yard. I asked how the burial had gone. "Fine." Then she added. "And, they had a piper."

And you try and tell the young people of today that ..... they won't believe you.

I remember my grandfather telling about how he and his brother went to a dance up in Broughton in Furness. This was a bike ride of seventeen miles there and seventeen miles back.
(I've done it myself, but didn't dance when I got there!) Anyway they were almost home and it was late (or early depending on how you look at these things). My grandfather commented to his brother that it was 4am, so they might get an hour in bed before their father woke them up to start milking.
They got home and found father sitting in the kitchen putting his boots on. His only comment was 'well you'll be no good for anything today so we'd better get a good start.' So they didn't get to bed that night.
Now I've no tales like that to recount. I was far too sensible, and soon discovered that 'I've got to milk tomorrow morning' was a perfectly acceptable excuse to leave early when the evening was getting tedious.
In fact, milking got me out of at least one school detention. The teacher who taught us French was keeping us in for an extra hour after the 3:45pm finish because some of the class had been messing about. Anyway I didn't say anything, just packed my bag and quietly walked out. He stopped me at the door and asked where I was going. I replied "I'm going home to milk. My dad has gone to a farm sale and I promised I'd get home in good time to make a start. So be so good as to take this up with him." He stood opened mouthed as I bade him a courteous good day and left. I suppose it isn't an excuse you get from many fourteen/fifteen year olds

Another time, way back when I was about eight, I remember my dad collecting me from school. Now this just didn't happen, and what's more he turned up with a tractor and trailer. 'How cool is that?' I mean anyone can travel by car.

It turns out that they were baling. The knotters on the baler were slightly out of alignment. The first bale was tied perfectly, the second well enough, but the third bale wasn't tied at all. But if you hit the knotter 'just there' with a hammer, just after it had tied the second bale, then it tied the next bale perfectly.

Now Alan Armer (Our local agricultural engineer) would have had a mechanic out to fix it within minutes of being phoned. But fixing the knotters would have taken an hour and rain was promised. So the field was baled by having me sit on the back of the baler with a hammer. First bale tied perfectly, second bale tied well enough, clunk with the hammer, First bale tied perfectly, next bale tied well enough, clunk.

But thinking back this wasn't my only contribution. In the same year, still aged about eight, I was sitting on the seat of the MF135 when we were carting straw. Grandfather put the tractor in low gear. I was there to steer and men would throw bales up to my grandfather on top of the trailer. If he wanted the tractor to stop he'd shout 'Whoa'. I'd get off the seat and stand on the clutch (at the age of eight I couldn't reach the clutch peddle from the seat). When he wanted the tractor to move off again he'd shout 'Hod' and I'd get off the clutch, go back to the seat and concentrate on the technical details of steering.

Funnily enough when I tell some of these stories people look horrified. But think about it. How many eight year olds feel valued and part of the team? Feel they're making a genuine contribution to the family business?

Anyway it was all worth it just for the expression on the face of the French master.

Beach cobbles and courtesy

It's a lot of years ago now when I come to think of it. But on one side of our meadow gate, leading into the yard, there was a low wall. It was made of beach cobbles, (think rustic rubble) and cement. The only thing of real interest was that one of the stones was a reasonably substantial piece of sandstone; substantial enough that the Ordnance Survey had cut one of their benchmarks into it.

Anyway it was just one of those things that you have lying about. We didn't think a lot about it. Life went on. Anyway at a farm sale we'd picked up a three ton trailer for about a fiver. It wasn't in particularly good condition but really we got it for one specific job, it did the job and was then parked in the meadow out of the way.

Then suddenly we had another job for it. I yoked it onto the tractor and towed it out of the meadow gate. A piece of the trailer floor was sticking out and was going to catch on the wall, but the floor was rotten, and if it broke off, it'd save me having to cut it off, so this wasn't a problem. Except when it caught the end of the wall it pulled about five feet of the wall down, the wood remained determinedly unbroken. Of course, in the five feet of wall that had collapsed was the piece of sandstone with the benchmark on it.

Anyway I doubtless muttered something and went and got on with whatever I was doing. Next time it was fine and I had a free couple of hours (which might not necessarily have been the same year) I rebuilt the wall up again. Now I don't know if you've ever had to work with beach cobbles, but it isn't like building with bricks. They sort of go together but you have to work with them, not against them. As a result of this, when the bench mark went back into the wall, it was probably three feet to the left and four feet higher than it had been when whoever it was had cut it.

This wasn't, in our eyes at least, a problem. Indeed we thought no more about it. The wall had come down, the wall had been fixed, end of story. Except that some years later some bloke wanders into the yard with a lot of surveying kit, and proceeds to start doing measurements. These involve him checking the benchmark. Repeatedly. Now I don't know about you, but if I go into a place and there's someone there, I say 'hello'. I may have a right to be there, I may have a duty to be there, but common courtesy dictates that if you traipse across someone's yard and garden, you do at least say 'hello' and perhaps even explain what you're doing.

Well I worked out that he must be from the Ordnance Survey or some vaguely affiliated body from stuff he had in his car. But he ignored both my dad and myself, and just walked up and down our yard doing repeated measurements and repeated calculations. At regular intervals he came back to the benchmark and recalculated all over again.

As we had a brew and watched him out of the window, I did ask my dad if we should bring him up to date with the new situation, but dad said that if the bloke was too ignorant to say 'Good Morning' then he was obviously too ignorant to be worth dealing with. So we didn't bother. Anyway after quite some time the bloke drove away and we never saw him again, and no one else said anything about it, so perhaps he fudged the figures. Who knows? Then again, if they do finally come to check, they'll have problems. The wall has long gone, there is a building there and today is the first time in more than ten years I've even thought about the incident. And I haven't a clue where we put that lump of sandstone.

Easter people?

Someone once told me if I had something to say, blog it. I suppose it's pithier than telling me to drop it down into an abyss of forgotten electrons where it'll sink without trace until it comes to rest far from sight or memory.
But you know this winter we've been having? I mean the one we're having now, not the one we had last month. Well just north of us there are people in deep trouble, or rather deep snow.
The gales meant the snow drifted and sheep, huddled behind hedges for shelter, were buried. Whilst it's happening there isn't much you can do. Go out into the blizzard to try and help and you'll probably die as well.
So as soon as the wind drops, you go out to try and rescue them. But of course the ground is covered in snow, it's colder than charity and you don't know where they are (because they're buried), you just know from past experience (your own or handed down) where they might be.
There's only so long they can survive. Not only that but last summer was rubbish, and so was the fodder a lot of people were able to make. And because it was wet, shepherds and their sheep have been fighting a fierce battle against liver-fluke. So this 'spring,' sheep are not in as good a condition as you'd hope
So by now, those sheep that were trapped are dead. But that isn't the end of it. Firstly they'll be finding dead sheep through to June as the snow melts. (Big drifts take a lot of shifting up on the fell.) Then there's the financial implications, no sheep, no income. To replace the sheep costs money. Lose a hundred sheep; it will cost you over £10,000 to replace them. Not only that but thanks to EU regulation, you cannot just bury them when you find them, you've got to pay a knacker £50 to take each one away.
Given that Oxfam in a survey last year found that a lot of hill farmers are living below the poverty line on less than £8,000 a year, then that money will take a lot of finding.

But I went for a walk today, looking for grass, because whilst we haven't got snow, we've got ewes with lambs who need feeding. Because it's Good Friday and one local church has got a series of displays telling the Easter Story, I dropped in. What really struck me was a painting, done yesterday, by a lady who had been showing a school class round and when they left, she felt she had to do something, and for her, this meant paint.

So there is this new painting, of a piece of rough hill country. To someone round here, it's obviously fell country she's painted, the sort of land you get up on Corney and across to Birker. And on this fell are three stark crosses. And the sky behind the crosses is stormy, but the lower sky is white as if there's a great tranche of snow about to burst forward over you as you look at the picture.

And to me that picture sums up the sort of pain, stress, and suffering that the people up the coast from us are suffering.

But it's Easter, and I suppose the other thing is that there's also the one who said 'I am the Good Shepherd' and I think he'll understand what these folk are going through at the moment.

Smarter than the average sheep. (And quite bright for a Londoner as well)

Sheep aren't the most stupid of God's creatures; they're not even the most stupid mammal. Indeed Horses could well have been created to allow sheep to feel that smug glow of intellectual superiority that everyone needs from time to time.

Not that this is high praise. There are single celled creatures floating in seas of freezing ammonia, illuminated by the dying suns of decayed nebulae who have more idea what is going on that your average horse. But who needs intelligence when you've got charisma and a good body? It's worked for horses and it'll doubtless work for others.

But I digress. Our next door neighbour had an issue with sheep. She's a retired lady and a Londoner by birth, but much to her joy has found herself living surrounded by sheep and lambs. Oh and remember, when I say next door, she is the nearest house in that direction, but it's a five minute walk, so we don't see her every week. But anyroad up, she was heading for bed the other night when she thought, 'That sheep sounds a little close.'

So she stepped out into her middle garden, and there, dancing along the top of the wall was a young lamb. This isn't too improbable as her garden is well below field level and the wall top isn't much higher than the field. Anyway, this was (briefly) cute, until the lamb fell off the wall and landed in the garden. At this point her quiet evening erupted into chaos as the lamb frantically tried to get back up the wall to join mother and mother tried to come down the wall to rejoin lamb.

Now at this point I can tell you, with all the confidence of a professional, that the thing to do is to catch the lamb, (which was probably about fifteen kilos), and then bodily hoik it over the wall.

What you don't do is to do what my neighbour did, which is to go into the house, get a kitchen chair, place chair against the wall and pat the chair indicating that the lamb jump onto the chair and then over the wall.

This never works. Sheep just aren't mentally equipped to cope with this sort of thinking. Their grasp of spatial geometry just isn't up to it. I'm glad our elderly border collie wasn't there to watch this. Border collies can convey baffled condescension better than any other species I've ever come across.

But she got the chair, placed it appropriately, attracted the lamb's attention to it, stood back and watched.

The lamb jumped onto the chair and then straight over the wall where it rejoined frantic mum.

Smarter than your average sheep obviously.

Was it love or just wind?

It's an interesting thing to have on your CV. If I lie on my stomach in the muck, my arms are just long enough to reach into the icy 'water' and pass a rope under the chest of a black limi heifer who has managed to get herself into a slurry pit.

It's one of these jobs you do methodically. First a cow-band round her neck, fasten it to the chainlink fence, now she's less likely to drown. Cattle float and can swim, but if they get tired, eventually their heads sink and they drown.

Next get the rope. Strip to the waist, all the while thanking the Lord that it wasn't a fortnight ago, and lie down in wind-dried muck.

Then quietly, because you don't want to upset her, slide your hand down one side of her shoulders, push the end of the rope under her and grab it with your other hand.

Fasten rope, attach rope to fore-end loader, lift, pull back and deposit one wet and exhausted heifer on dry land.

With heifer washed off with warm water, stomach tubed with electrolytes and wrapped in straw out of the wind, you finally get a chance to work out how she did it. If she'd broken through there, across that bit, and got a decent run up, she might just have been able to clear that fence there, which would have meant she'd have come down just here and then it's straight through the crust and into the disagreeable liquid below.

Before you get to the stage of structural modifications you begin to ask questions like, 'What on earth possessed her to do it?' Last night was a howling gale, perhaps something spooked her? Either that or looking at her age perhaps it's her first time abulling?

Well she won't be the first lass to end up in deeper waters than she expected on a first date.

Anyhow it wasn't how I'd intended to start my morning, but as they say, 'If you want to hear God laugh, tell him what you plan to do tomorrow.'

It must be spring, this evening I was nice to a poet.

Well it's about time. I mean by that it's about time that it was spring. (I don't think being nice to poets ought to be seasonal, it lures them into complacency.)
People were beginning to wonder whether it was going to show up at all, or whether we were going to do what we did last year, have two weeks of summer early then go straight into autumn.
At last we've got the first signs of grass, there's this hint of green. Indeed if I'm not smart enough to work out an excuse for putting a few ewes on the lawn I might even have to get the lawn mower out. So yes, spring might be happening, and about time too.
I've been helping out a bit with FCN, or the Farm Community Network (http://www.fcn.org.uk/) and you soon realise that some people have been finding it tough. In Cumbria we haven't had a decent summer for two years, I've talked to folk who last year got less than half the fodder they needed to carry their dairy herd through the winter, and they've been forced to buy in feed. I know families where each month since Christmas they've spent more than their annual profit on feed alone. So each month winter has continued, they've gone another year into debt. By January, they knew they'd make no money this year. By the start of February, next year was a bust as well. Anyway I'm sure you can get the picture, I'm not going to labour the point.
But now, at last, it feels as if spring is here. To be honest, it's my favourite time of year. Yes, summer's OK, autumn with the colours can be spectacular, especially when you get up into the Lake District. But it's spring which shows this area off to perfection.

What I really love is when you look round and see a million different shades of green, each subtly different, and as the sun moves, they all change. I don't think anywhere in the world does spring half as well as England, and to be honest, nowhere in England does spring half as well as Furness.

Looks like it's probably time I got the puncture fixed on my pushbike; it seems that I might need it again. Frankly this winter, when it wasn't raining it was blowing a gale, so the bike stayed carefully put away and the front tyre was a job I'd get round to. But spring is here, life is starting, lambs are putting good taste and dignity to one side and are gambolling. I walked down one track and the air was heavy with the scent of gorse. (A lady of my acquaintance waxed lyrical at this point, "The smell of the gorse! It's like pina colada! Do you know the old saying, 'When the gorse is in flower, kissing's in season.'?" As you know, any time of year you can usually find a bit of gorse in flower.) Not only the gorse, but the blackthorn is in bloom and the bird song can be deafening at times. We've done it, we've lived through another winter, we're out the other side, we've won another year for ourselves.

Oh yes, and I mentioned poets. I bet you never realised that farmers are very like poets. You see, neither farmers nor poets can honestly claim to be involved in an economic activity.

Occasionally you get it right.

Not sure why the incident came to mind, perhaps it was seeing the honeysuckle.

It isn't even flowering yet but it started me thinking about scents and the way scents seem to be able to tap straight into your memories. Catch a whiff of a long forgotten scent and suddenly you're transported right back to childhood.

It seems to surprise people but in fact I've got a good sense of smell. I can have a flock of sheep walk past me on the lane and sometimes catch the suggestion that they've got blowfly problems. Whether it's acetone on the breath of a milk cow, or the hint of retained cleansing, it's a diagnostic tool I've found useful over the years.
But there are real pleasures to be had. The other day I walked through a dell that was almost full of gorse bushes in flower. The smell of gorse, (some people describe it as being like vanilla) was almost overwhelming.
But it's honeysuckle that I remember best. It'll be about fifteen years ago now; we had some stock escape late one evening. It'd be about midnight when we discovered this and everybody got dressed and went out to get them rounded up again. An hour and a half later we'd got them all back, or so we thought. We'd stuck them in a building to calm down and counting dark cattle in a dark building doesn't really inspire confidence in the final number you come up with.
So I'd just check one last place where they might be. Everybody went back to bed and I walked down one track round the back of the hill to make sure there weren't any cattle down there. It was a bright moonlight night and the air was still. As I trudged along the track I turned a corner and stepped into a pool of honeysuckle. The scent hung in the air, so rich and thick I almost had to cut my way through it. I've never smelled it like that before and I don't suppose I'll experience it again, but occasionally, by accident, you can be in the right place at the right time. Every so often you get it right.

Dogs, dreams and fairy tales.

On Tuesday our current working dog, young Sal, got her first real go at working cattle on her own, without quad bikes or other people to fret about. I discovered that she has the same cattle technique as old Jess had. When moving cattle, first go to the front end, snap at their nose to tell them that you're the boss and expect action. I think of it as the 'Granny Weatherwax' school of management which boils down to 'If you haven't got respect, you've got nothing'. (For those of you who don't know Granny Weatherwax; read Wyrd Sisters.)
Anyway yesterday Sal was working with me, moving some sheep. She did that OK and then heard the quad bike. She spotted that the quad bike was also moving sheep pretty effectively and she immediately ignored the sheep and started herding the quad bike, just to make sure that it kept working and didn't slouch off or stop for some reason.
Now way back, I'd be still at school; we were hay-timing and the baler broke a shear bolt. Not an uncommon thing to happen. But everything stops; my father and my uncle unjam the baler and put in a new shear bolt. During this process, old Ben, our working dog at the time, sat and observed. (Working Border Collies don't merely watch; that is a passive activity. They observe because they somehow give the impression that they're valued participants in the activity which wouldn't go well without their input.)
Finally, everything fixed, my father started the tractor, and as it moved off old Ben darted in to give the baler wheels a nip, just to get it going and make sure it kept working.
Now I'm second to none in my appreciation of the Border Collie. They regularly give the impression of absolute certainty. They know, to the very core of their being, that they are the professionals, and I'm just some ape descendant with an opposed thumb who thinks he knows something about moving livestock. There are times when I'm vaguely honoured that I'm considered worthy to discuss policy with.

But even Border Collies have their limits. There are things which are beyond their comprehension; things that they don't really understand. They cope with them; they just treat them as sheep.

Old friend, a biography of a border collie.

It was sixteen years ago that I decided we'd better get a pup to work alongside Boz who was our working dog at the time. Boz had reached late middle age and even border collies don't work forever.

It was probably Nancy who told me who had a litter of pups bred from working parents. I phoned to check they still had some and drove across to see them. There were two pups left. A dog pup who somehow reminded me of a pyjama dog; pick him up and he just flopped affectionately all over you. At the same time there was a small bitch pup who came across to see what was going on, was bright, intelligent and interested. So I picked her, named her Jess, paid £45 which is the only time in my life I've ever paid for a dog, and fetched her home. I was told later that her brother made a local family a great and much loved family pet.

Got her home, bathed and deloused her and after a couple of weeks she was moved out of the house and into a home of her own, next to Boz. The presence of Boz probably explained why, all her life, she'd try to hide food by burying it, pushing stuff over it with her nose. She once buried a dead lamb in straw whilst I was talking to someone and it took five minutes to find the damn thing again.

Jess started working milk cows. This is good training for a work dog; you're at it twice a day, every day, pretty much doing the same thing every time. She was good at it, a bit shy of strangers, a bit wary of other dogs but a great player with children. She'd been with us for six months with Boz getting more and more confused until, as if someone had flicked a switch, he suddenly grasped the whole play concept and really threw himself into it. I think she gave him a whole new lease of life.

I also remember my daughter and her two cousins deciding they'll tire Jess out so she'd sit quietly. The idea was that one of the three children would run about, then when they felt tired, one of the others would run about, then the third would take over and the first two would get a rest. It didn't work.

In 1999 we gave up milking cows. The price we were being paid for milk dropped to 14 pence per litre and I decided that dairy farming had become an expensive hobby, more expensive and wetter than racing ocean going yachts but with less social cachet.

Anyway we shifted to suckler cows, and then bucket reared calves, with cattle sold as store for others to fatten. Jess took to this with no trouble at all. She had absolute self-confidence, she'd happily work cattle in a yard, even fetch them out of a building, which takes a dog with strong nerves.

Then as time moved on, we started farming alongside Matt and his sheep. Sheep came as something of a revelation to Jess. It took her a full half hour to get her head round the fact that they were now her problem. Watching her watching them it was as if she was mentally flicking through the manual, and then the moment of revelation, she realised that 'sheep' was the default setting.

Her technique always reminded me of Granny Weatherwax from Terry Pratchett's Discworld series. Granny Weatherwax always held that "If you haven't got respect, you haven't got anything." Certain all livestock on the farm were expected to respect her.

I remember one time Matt and I were fetching ewes and lambs home down the lane. One lamb would keep darting back down the lane, heading back for the field. Nell, Matt's dog, would shoot off after it, turn it, and bring it scampering back. This happened three or four times. On the final time this happened, the lamb chose to make its break when Jess happened to be in there when it turned round to make a run for it. Her jaws snapped shut just in front of the lamb's nose. It stopped, looked at her, turned back round and trotted docilely along with the rest.
Another time we had a bunch of someone else's heifers get into one of our fields. We arranged to give them a day or so to calm down, then the neighbour would turn up with plenty of people, I'd get them out of the field onto the road, and he'd have enough people to move them along the road and away. No problem. Jess and I bring them up the field towards the gate. At that point one of them turned in the gateway and started that stiff legged walk that can turn almost instantly into a run. Any minute and the whole lot would be off and we'd have it all to do again. Jess just walked up to the lead heifer and stood in front of it. The heifer stopped, somewhat surprised, and brought its nose down to sniff the dog in front of it. Jess snapped her teeth together so close to the nose the heifer must have felt the draught. The heifer backed off a little, looked again at the dog, decided that suddenly it wasn't fun any more, turned and led the others quietly out of the gate and onto the main road.
Jess just swaggered casually after them. If you haven't got respect, you've got nothing!
Jess had her weaknesses. She hated fireworks. We ended up fetching her into the house on bonfire night after one occasion when she'd slipped her collar and disappeared for three days.

She also disliked the internal combustion engine. A quad bike was OK; it allowed humans to move at a sensible speed. But she loathed riding in cars. One time we had some cattle on some land rented away. I thought it would be nice for her to look stock somewhere new. But when I came to put her back in the car, she disappeared. She was gone for about four days until the person whose land it was phoned to say he'd seen her and shut her in a barn. I was passing with a tractor and cattle trailer and dropped in to collect her. She'd already escaped from the barn but when she saw me she was pleased to see me and came over and allowed me to carry her into the tractor cab with me. On the way home she started off in the left foot-well. She climbed up onto the left window seat, wormed her way behind me to the right window where she sat on top of the hydraulics, down into the right foot-well, up onto the dash, then down into the left foot-well again. She'd nervously made three circuits of the tractor cab, looking totally stressed out, by the time I got her home.

She had a large area that she called hers. She'd wander it when she was 'off duty'. One time at the farm next door the lady of the house had sat down to watch the TV in the comfort of her own front room. She put her hand down to pick up the TV guide from beside her chair and instead found Jess who'd wandered in and was just sitting companionably next to her.

She wasn't a big one for playing with balls and suchlike. Colin our vicar at the time was a bit worried that his dog (which had Border Collie in it) might take to chasing sheep. So he fetched his dog down and we took the two dogs into the field with some sheep. I had Jess gather the sheep and the other dog looked on totally impassive. Colin then threw the ball and his dog sprang into action, almost knocking Jess over to get to it. She just watched with incomprehension as this other dog played with a ball.

When Matt arrived with his three dogs, they were working dogs but also would play with a ball. I'd kick the ball, Matt's three dogs would pile in and chase it, and Jess would run with them, avoiding the ball but barking enthusiastically at the others, without contributing anything to the operation. She'd probably invented management.

By the time she was thirteen she still didn't look much older than a dog of six or seven, but it was then she was struck by a hit and run driver on the main road near the church. Some other motorist saw her, phoned the police who phoned a vet who turned up just before I did. We got her to the surgery where he gave her an assortment of injections and they kept her in for a couple of days. When she came home, there had been nerve damage to her left front leg which just didn't work, and she'd probably suffered some slight damage to her hips.

At this point it was decided that she could no longer sleep in her cattle trailer, but had better move into the house at least until she'd recovered or not. But she recovered. Her left front leg never healed, so had to be amputated, but she took that in her stride. With only three legs she wasn't really up to working cattle and sheep any more, she'd lost the unthinking self-confidence, and she decided she was retired.

Anyway she managed another three years. Her retirement consisted of living in the house, snoozing by the fire in winter (she approved of fire) and walking miles with me looking stock and generally keeping an eye on things. When I went back to doing more writing, she'd often lie behind me, keeping an eye on things and making sure everything was done to a standard a border collie would consider suitable.

Finally last week she started to look unwell. Her appetite went which wasn't like her. So we took her to the vets on Saturday and they diagnosed a major womb infection. They gave her some injections but on Sunday she was no better. To deal with the infection it would take a major operation, the removal of her womb. Frankly she was no longer up for it. At the same time, the hip damage she'd suffered in the car accident had become arthritis and she was finding walking difficult. So yesterday, at the age of almost seventeen, she went to her final rest.

I don't know if anyone has seen 'The Power of the Dog' by Rudyard Kipling? The older I get the more I appreciate Kipling.

> When the body that lived at your single will,
> With its whimper of welcome, is stilled (how still!),
> When the spirit that answered your every mood
> Is gone - wherever it goes - for good,
> You will discover how much you care,
> And will give your heart to a dog to tear!

Four lesbians in a fast car

Over the years I've avoided equine entanglements. I used to boast that I'd eaten horse more recently than I'd ridden one, but now thanks to Tesco pretty well everyone can say that.

Still I've avoided going into the whole 'livery yard' diversification thing. Not through innate conservatism or immense wisdom but basically because I'd heard too many stories.

One lass I knew did Livery for a few years. She had tales to make your eyes water. As she said, "I didn't mind helping them organise their show timetables, but be damned if I was going to help them organise their adultery as well."
She also got fed up of having to cough loudly before going into her own barn, in case she might stumble on something (or in one case quite literally stumble over something) that she'd prefer not to know about.
One lady brought a horse in for livery. Things went well enough for three months or so but then the rent started falling behind. My informant made tentative enquiries (she's very English you know, doesn't want to make a fuss) and discovered that the horse was owned by the husband and the livery fees were being paid by the boyfriend. The two gentlemen in question had at this point discovered each other's existence and were less than happy with the situation. The lady who had brought the horse in had more chance of becoming the next Pope than she had of paying the bill.
At this point my informant had had enough. She parked a tractor across the stable door and took the back wheels off. She didn't care who paid her but someone was going to before they could get their horse back.
Which sort of brings us to the title of this piece; another place and time has moved on. Now in these ostentatiously enlightened times a (different) lady of my acquaintance doing livery discovered that adultery had also moved on. She had a female client who had a horse with her. As far as I can make out the husband was paying for the horse and the lady and her girlfriend were both riding it. And when said lady decided to go off with girlfriend and abandon husband, husband of course stopped paying.
So as usual these things get acrimonious and people get all upset. People forget themselves and make threats because they aren't willing to take responsibility for their own actions. After all it's easier to do that than try to put things right.

Eventually I became peripherally involved. I was walking quietly down the lane minding my own business when this car came past me rather quickly. I stepped promptly to the side and had just recovered my equilibrium when my informant appeared in her car to ask me a question which I'm unlikely to forget. "Have you just seen four lesbians in a fast car?"

The horseman's word

Every craft has its secrets, the tips it passes down through the generations. Now I'm the generation that never had to work horses, but my father had over twenty years of working them.

Back then the big work horses were pretty well trained and as they were worked most days they tended to be used to being handled and they were used to being driven and to following instruction.

Now, an awful lot of the horses you see about are rarely handled. Yes someone will come in every day and feed them, check their water, and perhaps even groom them. But whereas the old work horse would be harnessed and worked six days a week, a lot of riding horses now might not be ridden every weekend. So frankly a lot of horses now are pretty idle and poorly behaved.

What brought this to mind was remembering a conversation I had with a chap perhaps ten or fifteen years older than me, one lunch time in Ulverston Auction Mart. He'd been working with an old chap who had been a horseman back in the days before tractors. They'd driven up the lane to get to a field to fix a gap, and they'd passed this lady struggling to get her pony into her horse box. Half an hour later, the gap fixed, they drove back and she was still struggling to lead it into the horse box.

The old lad stopped the tractor and said to my informant, "Let's get her loaded."

The pony would walk up to the foot of the trailer ramp, put its front hooves on the bottom of the ramp and then refuse point blank to go any further. A not very large lady struggles to physically manhandle a fat pony up a ramp.
So the old horseman took over. He had my informant stand on one side of the pony's head, the lady on the other, told them to speak nicely to it whilst he pushed gently.
My informant held the lead rope, but had his hand on the halter by the pony's cheek and was trying to get it to budge by speaking nicely to it. To be fair, the pony seemed to appreciate this but was still not moving. The lady owner was listening carefully to everything he was saying, just in case she learned anything. Then suddenly the pony shot forward, straight up the ramp and into the trailer. They hastily shut the gates and got the ramp up before it changed its mind. The lady, genuinely grateful, thanked them and drove off. My informant turned to the old horseman and asked, "So what did you do."
"Well lad, when you get an 'orse like that as won't move, grab a handful of nettles in your cap and lift its tail with your other hand. Then slap its arse with the nettles."
There are some things they don't teach you in college.

The third great lie.

You know the three great lies?
- The cheque is in the post.
- Of course I'll still love you in the morning.
- I'm from the government and I'm here to help you.

And I'm sitting here waiting for the government 'help line' (no fantasy writer would have dared use the level of irony implied by the term 'help line') to tell me how a self-employed person claims sick pay for a fortnight.
On Friday I sat and listened to it for 45 minutes. Today I've got the speaker phone on so I can get on with something else.

Oh yes, a voice. "Thank you for waiting, please continue to hold and we will answer your call as soon as possible. Or you may prefer to ring back later. Our opening times are from 8am to 6pm, Monday to Friday."

And now back to the Vivaldi. What did he ever do to get himself involved in the 'Help line' industry?'

Still while I'm waiting I can tell you a story someone reminded me off earlier today.

Way back, when I were a lad (This is the local equivalent of 'Once upon a time' so bear with me) I went to the local grammar school. One morning a couple of lads my own age approached me and asked if I could get hold of ammonium nitrate.

"No problem, how much would you like?"

"How much does it cost?"

"Well my dad pays about £100 a ton for it. It comes in hundredweight bags." (To be honest I've forgotten the 1968 price of ammonium nitrate).

"Oh we don't need that much."

"How much do you want?"

"Oh about this much." (Gesturing with cupped hands.)

"We've got a torn bag; I'll get you some from that."

Next morning I arrive with a couple of pounds of ammonium nitrate in a plastic bag. We worked out the pro-rata price assuming £100 a ton, rounded up slightly, and they went on their way rejoicing. Keep the customer satisfied, that's what it's all about.

A week or so later my father gets a phone call. Apparently these two lads had made various bangs on waste ground and a 'concerned parent' had contacted the headmaster. The headmaster had been so troubled he'd decided to contact my parents immediately rather than have me summoned to his office. So he phoned, and lucky for me, got my dad. (When I say lucky for me, my mum was a teacher and tended to regard some things as much more serious than my dad did.)

The headmaster said (I loosely paraphrase) "Did you know your son was selling Ammonium nitrate to other boys who are causing explosions."

My dad's reply, "Well I hope he's getting more for it that I'm paying for it."
And that killed it. Dead. At this point the headmaster probably realised that the sale of ammonium nitrate wasn't illegal and probably wasn't even against school rules.
Nothing was said to me until some weeks later when my dad remembered
And when he remembered about the phone call, he told me about the bangs he and his mates had made when he was a lad. I have always been proud of my dad.
Wonder how many different security services picked up on this blog post?

Computers, politicians and pig slurry

A lot of years ago now I was in the 5th form at school (This is in the good old days before they changed everything to year ten or whatever) and we had, believe it or not, a careers master who would talk to us.

Admittedly he was a maths master who did careers as well but he was keen, and obviously had a mate working in the field because we were used as the guinea pigs when they tested a 'computerised careers questionnaire.' Really that should be in flashing lights or at least italic because no one had heard of them before.

Anyway I did the questionnaire along with the other ninety lads in the year and thought no more about it; until I was called back in to answer a question that had been troubling them.

The format, if I remember it properly, was the questions were in the form of 'would you prefer to do x or y.' This doubtless made the answers easy to put into the computer (remember this is a 1970s computer) and they were comparatively easy to answer. There was one small issue which had brought me to their attention. The question was, "Would you prefer to clean out pigs or look after old people?" I, alone of all those who had filled in this questionnaire had answered, "Clean out pigs."

Because this question was apparently to calibrate the system and ensure that those filling it in were being serious and could read etc, the guy whose project it was really wanted to see me. What he discovered was that I had read the question, pondered it carefully and then, based on my knowledge and experience, answered it.

After all, I knew that cleaning out pigs tended to be a high pressure hose job, done in working hours, sometimes preceded by a quick pass or two with a tractor loader to get rid of the heavy stuff. Looking after old people was constant, hard, demanding work; often thankless, often unending and normally unsocial.

The problem is that the questioner had written his question without any real comprehension of the nature of the alternatives he'd included in his question. What he had been thinking was 'clean out pigs' equals dirty disgusting back breaking work. On the other hand was 'looking after old people' cuddly, virtuous, socially desirable. Pity about the reality, yet I was the only person who was apparently grounded in the reality.

What set this off was someone said that they felt that David Cameron should be put to cleaning out pig sties. Firstly there aren't any, or if there are it would be a doddle of a job because they'll be the proud property of smallholders with a cherished pig or two.

Secondly the last thing we need in one of the most efficient industries this country has is some untrained noddy wandering in and doing a job he isn't trained for.

If you doubt the efficiency, look at the farm gate prices. As I write, milk is about 24 pence a litre. We got 30 pence a litre back in 1996. (I use milk as an indicator because I know the prices without checking.) Perhaps civil servants could survive with their departments still on 1996 budgets. But it also showed (and I'm not picking on one person) how food production and the people involved in it, is regarded in this country. Agriculture is a suggested dumping ground, a gulag for politicians. I can think of no other class of people less suited to taking part in a real job where you have to take responsibility for your actions and own up when you screw up.

Oh, and the 'computerised careers questionnaire.' Well much to the surprise of our careers master, it said I ought to be a farmer or a journalist. I'm both simultaneously, and occasionally over the years I've often wished I could meet the guy who designed the system, just to tell him he got at least one right.

Creeping calmly towards Christmas.

You know it's a bad sign when normally sensible young women go shopping wearing Santa Hats. If they've got some poor bloke in tow as well then things are doubtless about to get stressful.

I walked into town today, not really to buy anything but just to shunt money about and make sure various other jobs had been done. So I didn't really call in any shops or spend any money, but it was interesting just to watch everybody else. A lot of people were cheerful, some looked a bit stressed. I did call in to one shop to pick up some pickled onions. (Living the dream here, we know how to do Christmas, and you need something to go with the cold meat.)

Talking to one of the lads stacking shelves and he commented that people had already started 'panic buying'. Given that the shops will be open this weekend, open the 24th, and open again on the 27th, it's not as if we were laying in provisions for a re-run of the siege of Troy.

What gets me about Christmas is the stress some people seem to inflict upon themselves. I'm afraid I'm past that now.

On two consecutive Christmas Days we had power cuts (but fortunately we cook using an oil fuelled Rayburn.) On the next Christmas the Rayburn ran out of oil on Christmas day at about 10am, but fortunately we had electricity that year.

The most 'exciting' Christmas for me was where we had a power cut on Christmas Day, we had a dairy cow who needed a caesarean on Boxing Day, and the day after that, as I was putting silage into the troughs for the milk cows, the tractor put a front wheel through the slats on the top of the slurry bit, breaking a concrete sleeper and toppled over slowly, stopping at an angle of 45 degrees, stuck. I had to phone someone with a telescopic handler who dropped round and lifted the front end up so I could back out. By this stage I'd had enough of the entire Christmas experience, especially as I was doing two men's work, but was paying someone to sit at home because I couldn't afford to pay double time for them to come in and help.

It was at that stage that we started redesigning the business to eliminate the need for paid staff.

I think Christmas needs to be put in its place. My mother was a teacher, she had Christmas 'up to here' at school in December, so Christmas started at home on the day after she broke up. So decorations went up on December 23rd and came down promptly on 12th night.

Christmas is a different festival from New Year. There are five working days between them. We always worked on the principle that if we couldn't contact a supplier between Christmas and New Year, we didn't need them during the rest of the year either.

And Christmas Day? A decent start, get stock fed, (we're no longer milking cows) if things go well might even make 9:30am service. Then after dinner, read and/or snooze, Queen's Speech, back outside to feed round again and check everything is OK before finishing in time for tea. Finish up with a relaxing evening with family.

After the first three thousand years we've about got it right.

It's winter, it isn't raining, and I've been laying a hedge again. (Round here we call them dykes, but if I write about laying dikes I'd probably crash google in the USA.)
But no, I've just finished laying a hedge that my grandfather never got round to. The weather has been atrocious, at times I've gone down when the wind's dropped, done the next length and hastily hammered stakes in and secured the laid hedge to them because otherwise they'd have been blown away.
And water? One reason for doing this length of hedge is that if I do, next door can clean the gutter out on his side and it'll drain both fields a bit and do a bit of good for both of us. It's not something new or contemporary; indeed it's something farmers will have been doing for at least three thousand years. Most of the tools haven't changed a lot, save that steel is probably better than bronze, and frankly a chainsaw is better than an axe for some jobs.
So buggerlugs here has been trimming elderly hawthorn with a chainsaw, dragging the stuff I've cleared out across the sodden ground, often in standing water nearly a foot deep. This is real agriculture, necessary, hard work and with no noticeable financial return.

Anyway it's done, and is fenced and sheep proof (if anything can be said to be sheep proof). Indeed we even had a couple of roe deer down the other evening, inspecting the results. Admittedly they cleared the whole lot with contemptuous ease but I'm not trying to fence in deer.
But because I've been busy, somehow I never got the blog done, which is a pity if you like bad taste jokes about laying dikes

Now you've got broadband, text me.

Some years ago, I got an email from a mate which said "Now you've got broadband, send me a text."
I just stared at the email on the screen of my desk top computer before finally emailing him back the one word, "Why?"
I'm afraid I couldn't understand his answer, but it seemed to boil down to 'because you can.'
I felt my comment still stood, 'Why?'
It's just that yesterday I was talking to a chap, he's a decent bloke, competent, useful, and if fate has led him to becoming an office wallah, it's not really his fault and nobody holds it against him.
He was saying how he'd ended up taking a fortnight's holiday because he hadn't managed to get all his days used up before the year end. The day his holiday started a farming friend of his was rushed into hospital with a suspected stroke.
Our office wallah showed his true mettle and for ten days out of the fourteen he worked full time (so we're talking about twelve hour days here,) alongside his friend's son and they pitched in and not merely kept everything fed, but got sheds cleaned out and tidied up so that when the friend came out of hospital (fortunately it wasn't a stroke) he didn't have any catching up to do.

The reason the chap mentioned this to me comes in the punch line. He said, "I had ten days mucking out sheds, feeding round, spreading slurry, and my phone never rang once. It was heaven."

Now I realise I'm really blessed in that we don't have a mobile phone signal here, so my phone, an elderly nokia, lives switched off in a drawer. If people want me, there's the land line.

When I go out, mostly I remember to take the phone and sometimes I even bother to switch it on. But it doesn't matter, if people want me, there's still the land line. If I'm out and they phone, my lady wife will take a message, and I'll get back to them on my return.

If I'm out and she's out, well try ringing later.

Why do people have to be able to be in constant in touch? Now I can see the advantage of a mobile phone. If I've got a problem, or I'm running late, then I can switch the phone on, ring home and let them know. Sometimes if I remember I'll leave it switched on, on the off chance home want to contact me (I don't think there's more than six people have the number.)

I have a friend whose use of the phone I admire. It's a genuine tool of his trade; he can see something in a charity shop or second hand shop, price it, buy it if it's worth buying and have it sold before he's even left the shop. That is something that he couldn't have done ten years ago.

His phone also holds an inordinate number of books so he always has something to read with him. This is possibly the one use that would tempt me to getting a more up-to-date phone. (Even nokias fail eventually, especially if they're jostling in your pocket with your car keys. At some point I'll have to bite the bullet and get a new one and this will probably happen within a decade.)

But at the moment my phone costs me about £15 a year on pay as you go, which isn't bad for a phone that cost £25 with £20 phone credit. Looking at the price of contracts for a 'decent' phone, I spend less a year than these contracts cost a month. You know what; I might just keep on sticking a paperback in my jacket pocket.

And the rain came down

Yep, it's wet. I got soaked to the skin taking some feed three hundred yards to a bunch of bullocks. The water is running down our drive like a river, and all in all, it's the start of the Cumbrian Summer Monsoon.
It's been wet for the last few days, on and off, but what struck me has been how dusty the ground is, just half an inch down.
But anyway, we've had a decent summer, it's still warm, grass is still growing and that is what matters.
It's funny, in spite of all my best intentions I've got dragged into discussions on the web about Israel and Gaza and all that sort of stuff.
I hadn't intended to, I firmly resolved to keep out of it. But you know what it's like, there's only so much asinine stupidity a chap can put up with without coming over all ironic.
I suspect it's the level we've degenerated to. It's no longer necessary to know anything about the subject any more. All that matters is that you have an 'opinion' and you're 'sincere' and that means you're right.

Bullocks!

Which brings me on to the other day. I dropped round to see friends. For environmental reasons Natural England want cattle grazing some of the fells. Fair enough, they're willing to cover the cost because it isn't really an economic activity. But because the fell has roads across it they want the cattle to have collars with fluorescent bands on them so that drivers, who might otherwise miss seeing half a ton of somnambulant bovine, might at least catch the flash of light as the occasional ray of Cumbrian sunshine falls on the collar.

So my friend was putting the collars on. This isn't quite as easy as you'd think. You've got to get the animal into the crush where its head is 'sort of held' and then you put the collar on. So I ended up putting the collar on as he put them in the crush, which made the job go faster.

And it was good to be back doing something I'm good at. Just burble away cheerfully to them, in a voice that lets them know that you're not worried so why should they be upset. Then as they stand there you carefully lean over them and gently put the open collar under their throat and charily fasten it. All the while being ready to drop everything and get out of the way if your honeyed words don't keep them pacified.

It went well. One memorable moment came when I was dealing with a limi heifer, to whom the technical term 'radged' might be applied. I got the collar on and opened the crush gate. She hurtled out of it, crossed the yard, still accelerating and shot out of the gate, only to stop abruptly when faced with over six thousand acres of fell.

After all what's the point in running madly, crashing through fences and making your break for freedom if the nearest fence is a bus ride away?

So outfaced by reality she stopped, stared at it and then wandered quietly off to join her mates.

Funny how many people cannot cope with the reality, when faced with it they just ignore it and wander of and stand with their mates, telling each other what nice people they are because they're 'sincere' which means they have to be right.

Me, I suspect I'd probably just stick to doing what I do best. Apparently this involves sticking collars on bullocks so sensible people can avoid them.

Dogging their heels

A new project traditionally goes through these phases.

Wild enthusiasm
Disillusionment
Confusion
Panic
Search for the guilty
Punishment of the innocent
Promotion of non-participants

When training a young border collie, you can pass through all seven phases in as little as twenty seconds.
Still one tries.
But on Saturday I noticed that we had a gap in a hedge and a bunch of lambs had got out. Now when I say lambs I don't want you to get to emotionally involved. It's September. We're not talking about anything cute and fluffy. We're talking about a bunch of forty kilo potential trouble makers who are as cute as a collection of fairground boxers out on the beer.
So I gathered together the tools of the trade. These comprised of a post to help plug the gap, a mel to drive the post in, and Sal, our young dog.
I went into the field the lambs were supposed to be in, Sal ranging about in front of me. The lambs left in the field collected in a defensive huddle in a far corner and Sal obeyed my strict instructions to stay reasonably near me and leave them alone. So far, so good, her training is progressing; the wild enthusiasm can be contained.
Then through the gap into the other field, the situation was complicated because the field contained a bunch of bulling heifers and a bull. Still, worry about details when we have to.

At this point I'd put Sal on a lead (OK a long piece of baler twine through her collar but it's virtually the same). I then walked towards the lambs. They saw me (and more importantly Sal) and went into a huddle.

I walked past the huddle which drifted off to one side to maintain a respectable distance from me (and of course Sal.)

At this point things were going well. Sal was obviously giving her attention to the sheep, there were signs of enthusiasm and interest but we didn't have any mad pulling at the lead etc. The bulling heifers and Bull had noticed I was there but I wasn't doing anything interesting so they continued to watch me.

Then I moved with Sal around the back of the bunch of lambs which drifted, nonchalantly, back towards the gap and stopped, watching us.

You could see the lambs assessing the situation.

"It's that dog."

"Yeah but she's on a lead."

"For how long?"

"She's on a lead."

"I can see her teeth."

"She's just smiling."

"There's an awful lot of teeth. She has them on the top and bottom of her jaw, and along the sides as well. Nobody should have that many teeth!"

At this point we move towards the lambs. Now with a trained dog there'd have been no lead and the dog would have calmly moved towards the lambs who'd have turned and scuttled through the gap.

However we have Sal. If I'd removed the lead at this point we'd probably have something which from the air would have looked more like somebody breaking up the reds at the start of a game of snooker. She'd have moved toward them at speed, the flock instinct would have collapsed and lambs would have gone in every direction.

So we keep moving towards them, with Sal on the lead moving from side to side as well as forward. The lambs continue to head nonchalantly for the gap and by the time Sal and I arrive, the last one is through and has joined the defensive huddle in the other field. It's already practicing its innocent expression.

So I fix the gap and Sal stands, ears pricked, watching the sheep who watch her back.

Finally, job done, I leave. I whistle and Sal, somewhat reluctantly, turns away from the lambs who have been carefully to give her no further excuse to intervene.

I leave the field, a remarkably self-confident dog ranging ahead of me, secure in the knowledge that she's done a good job.

Now you might ask what she'd done. But if she hadn't been there, the lambs would just have run round and round the field all day, secure in the knowledge that I was never going to catch them.

But place Sal in the picture and suddenly it's no fun anymore.

Border Collies just half curl that lip, drop into the crouch, and suddenly the sheep remember their proper role in the performance and move as directed.

Not so much flies as plummets

Shepherd: Birds is the key to the whole problem. It's my belief that these sheep are laborin' under the misapprehension that they're birds. Observe their behaviour. Take for a start the sheep's tendency to 'op about the field on their back legs. Now witness their attmpts to fly from tree to tree. Notice that they do not so much fly as... plummet. (Baaa baaa... flap flap... thud.) Observe for example that ewe in that oak tree. She is clearly trying to teach her lamb to fly. (baaaaa... thud) Talk about the blind leading the blind.

Tourist: Yes, but why do they think they're birds?

Shepherd: Another fair question. One thing is for sure, the sheep is not a creature of the air. They have enormous difficulty in the comparatively simple act of perchin'. (Baaa baaa... flap flap... thud.) As you see. As for flight its body is totally unadapted to the problems of aviation. Trouble is, sheep are very dim. Once they get an idea in their 'eads, there's no shiftin' it.

Tourist: But where did they get the idea from?

Shepherd: From Harold. He's that sheep over there under the elm. He's that most dangerous of animals, a clever sheep. He's the ring leader. He has realized that a sheep's life consists of standin' around for a few months and then bein' eaten. And that's a depressing prospect for an ambitious sheep. He's patently hit on the idea of escape.

Tourist: Well why don't you just get rid of Harold?

Shepherd: Because of the enormous commercial possibilities should he succeed.

(Courtesy of Monty Python)

It's a funny old world. You cannot rely on anything being as it used to be. Sheep flock together, it's part of what sheep do; except we had one that didn't. I first noticed it a couple of months ago. Went into the field with Sal to round up some lambs and they all run together and stand in a clump. The theory is that you then move that clump in the direction you want them to go.
If I'd been rounding them up using a quad bike that would have been how it went. Except that Sal, being a border collie, spotted one almost fat lamb that wasn't doing this. This lamb drifted quietly off to the side then ducked down under the bridge and there she hid, troll like, in the gloom.

Of course Sal followed her down, but we had an impasse. Lamb couldn't go further forward and Sal was inadvertently stopping her coming back.

So some muppet (me) had to go down the other side of the bridge to chase the daft beggar out, at which point Sal could take over and drive it back to the flock.

Except that the stupid little beggar decided to swim for it. Wearing a heavy woollen jacket!

So guess who had to haul it out?

Anyway I dragged it out, pulled it to the group and this time it went home with them.

Scroll on a couple of months. On Wednesday I went with Sal to bring in the fat lambs. We were going to sort out some who were ready for selling. And this lamb dived quietly into another hollow and hid. Again Sal spotted it and eventually we dragged it out, pointed it at the rest of the group, and it dived off to one side, headed for the beck in an attempt to drown itself again. This time I grabbed its back leg before it could get into the water, tied it to a fence post and went to find the others, who of course had all gone home anyway.

So leaving them and Sal (who had got to the stage of hysterical frustration with this lamb) at home, I went back for the last ewe lamb. Of course she wouldn't walk, indeed refused to even stand up. And if I didn't have her on a lead, she'd dive into the beck.

So eventually I picked her up and slung her over my shoulders and we walked home that way. She was put in a separate pen, was judged to be over 40kg and so went to mart with the others for whom mint sauce is a distinct possibility.

Funny old world

You know what they say, "The sooner you fall behind the more time you'll have to catch up."
Hopefully today it'll be right because I've spent most of it doing things that need doing but which weren't even to be considered when I bounded cheerfully out of bed this morning. (Before you ask, yes I am a morning person. Milking cows for thirty years can reset anybody's personal alarm clock.)
Still I was busy really. Had to check lambs, and whilst I was there I intended to cut some ivy that I'd noticed choking a tree and then I'd break up some logs and carry them back. Which all meant I had an axe with me, obviously.
And as I set off up the field this white van towing a trailer stopped and two chaps got out and walked into our yard. This isn't usual, or encouraged so I wandered back to find out what was happening. The felling axe clasped casually in one hand was a mere incidental detail.
As I passed their van I noticed cockles in the trailer. So if they're cocklers, they might not even speak English. Ah well. It's not an easy job cockling; it's a dangerous world out there
But they saw me and came back. This is where it's useful not to jump to conclusions. They were two biggish chaps, and they were seriously hacked off with a genuine grievance. They'd had a trailer nicked the previous night. Someone in a blue Landrover with a white top had driven off with it, and had gone down our lane.
Problem with this is that our lane isn't a dead end, you come out the other end and you can drive into town. Their trailer is probably somewhere in Barrow by now.
So if you know someone with a Blue Landrover who has just acquired a battered five to six foot trailer, with its drawbar replaced with heavy box section steel, and the back gate replaced by two sections of scaffolding pole, they've probably nicked it.

When I last saw them these two lads were going to the police and to have a word with various scrap yards in case someone tries to cash it in. But they were also going to have a quiet drive round various parts of town, just keeping their eyes open.
I hope they find their trailer, but I don't think they are disposed to be particularly forgiving of the person who took it.

The Irishness of the long distance runner

It's like the Irishman said when asked for directions, "Well to get there I wouldn't start from here."
I know just what he means. We live down a series of narrow (ish) lanes and they tend to be so quiet that when I go into a field to feed sheep I can leave the gate open blocking the road because nobody will come along.
Wherever you're going, I wouldn't start from here.
But that's not to say we don't have excitement and see strange and unusual things. Like the day the bus came through. But that's another story.
It's just that some years back my father and I were doing some hedging. In the local vernacular the technical term is 'laying a dike.' I've been warned about using that phrase. Apparently for some of our colonial cousins who no longer speak the old tongue in all its richness and purity it means something entirely different.
Needless to say I'm not adverse to pandering to the unlettered, and thus I will take time out from the tale to explain that 'laying a dike' is where you work your way along a hedge, partially cutting through and bending over each upright stem, to thicken it and ensure it remains a stock-proof barrier.

Anyway there me and my dad were, busy away, and along the lane comes a pack of runners. We nodded to them, friendly like, and they ignored us. I can only assume that for some people, expending effort on courtesy when you're striving for a dopamine high is counterproductive. Or perhaps they just don't mingle with the peasantry? Who knows, obviously I don't because they wouldn't talk to us. But there was one runner, at the back of the pack, who did wave back and say 'Good afternoon' in a broad Irish accent.

Anyway father and I thought nothing of it. Ignorance is common enough and you no longer get upset by the ostentatious display. We carried on working away, until, about half-an-hour later the runners passed us again; heading in the same direction. Now if they'd been coming back you could understand it. They'd run 'out' and now they were running 'back'; but in the same direction? Obviously whatever it was involved big laps.

And of course they ignored us again.

Except for the Irish lad who stopped, looked at us and said, "We've been past here before haven't we."

Neither my father nor I were going to lie to the lad, so we admitted he had. So he said, "And this isn't the road to Leece is it?"

We agreed with him that it wasn't the road to Leece.

"So which is the road to Leece?"

Admit it, I couldn't not say, "Well to get there I wouldn't start from here."

But we relented and gave him directions

He muttered something under his breath which might have been some ancient Irish charm for all I know and then he sprinted off after the pack. Five minutes later they appeared again, going 'back' this time.

And of course they all ignored us, except for the Irish lad, still at the back, who gave us a cheery wave.

Horsing around

A man in a cinema notices what looks like a horse sitting next to him.
"Are you a horse?" asked the man, surprised.
"Yes."
"What are you doing watching a film?"
The horse replied, "Well, I liked the book."

I've always loved the work of the cartoonist Thelwell. But once, just once, I felt I might be sitting on the edge of one of his cartoons.
He was better known for his pictures of small girls on fat ponies, but he also catered for what we might call the larger lady (I know that makes him sound like a manufacturer of structural hosiery, or garments noted for their 'firm underpinnings', but you know what I mean).
Our farm sits on a ninety degree bend in a quiet rural lane. At times it even warrants the term 'leafy'. So we regularly get horse riders going up and down it and they're not normally a problem.
But one winter's morning I was clearing up the silage face and making sure our dairy herd had plenty to eat. Some cows were watching me with what passes for eager anticipation amongst middle aged bovines. The rest were just waiting, which is something milk cows can do really well.
One was leaning on the gate, looking along the lane to see if anything more interesting was happening there.
And for once, there was. Two ladies rode down the lane towards our gate. These weren't chits of girls on ponies; these were serious ladies on proper horses.
The first horse trots happily past our gate, glances at the cow, metaphorically shrugs and ignores it.

The second horse sees the cow and comes to a halt. Whether or not it had ever seen a cow before I don't know but it wasn't impressed and wasn't willing to go past. The rider (you know, the one in charge) urged it onwards. There may even have been cheerful cries of encouragement, it's a few years back and memory fades. But the horse wasn't convinced. On the other hand, the cries and general kerfuffle attracted the attention of another cow. She joined the first one to see what was going on.
Obviously if one cow is bad, two are worse, and the horse was even less impressed. So the lady rider became even more strident in her demands that the horse move on.
The sole effect of this was that several more cows came to line the gate. Street theatre is rare in the bovine world and chances to enjoy it should be grasped enthusiastically.
With this the horse took a pace backwards. The other rider brought her horse back and endeavoured to display to the wary horse that there wasn't a problem.
More cows were enticed by this to leave their contemplation of me forking silage into a barrow and made their way to the gate. This was now lined, two deep, with interested dairy cows.
By now the horse that had previously passed the gate without turning a hair was having second thoughts. It started walking sideways to get away from the gate and the rider did technical stuff with the reins and issued verbal commands which merely attracted more cows.
The rider of the more recalcitrant horse decided to get firm, she had dismounted and was going to lead the horse past. The cows at the gate were now four deep and the horse was having none of it. She was, no doubt, a fine figure of a woman, but the horse was at least four times her weight. It took one step forward, thought better of it and took three back.

The language coming from the two riders was growing choice. It has to be admitted that milk cows are not entirely unused to hearing such terms. But as the volume, and to some extent the pitch, climbed higher, the rest of the herd abandoned me for the performance laid on for them at the other side of the gate. Indeed our cows were now drawn up so deep at the gate that those at the rear couldn't see and there was considerable ill-mannered jostling going on at the back.
At this point the two horses decided that enough was enough. Walking sideways and/or backwards they determinedly headed away from the gate. Their riders remounted and rode, grim faced, back the way they had come.
Me? 'Tarbaby, he said nothing'.
Had I appeared it was only ever going to be my fault.
But apropos of nothing in particular, it is probably experiences like this that made me the man I am today.

Coffee, sheep, tractors, fine literature and bad rock'n'roll

Yesterday my lady wife and I were following a tractor and hedge-cutter down a lane. She commented that it didn't look like a desperately exciting job. My reply was along the lines that tractor driving wasn't at all exciting. Obviously when things go wrong it can get far too exciting but when done properly it can be a case of chugging along, working long hours and surviving on coffee and with bad rock'n'roll coming out of the radio.
But this morning I discovered that the task had been so soporific that the driver using the hedge-cutter had casually chopped through an old gate that we had used to block a gap. This reopened the gap and over a hundred ewes had wandered through to see what the wider world had to offer.

So I blocked the gap and went to bring the ladies back. This involved me chasing them through the gate and out of one field, onto the lane, and then taking them down the lane through another gate and back into their original field. Both gates opened to block the lane so it was a job I could do on my own.

This was lucky, because these ladies are heavily pregnant. Thus they are pampered. The dog isn't allowed anywhere near them in case she is a little bit too firm or things get too excitable. Everything is done nicely and quietly and gently.

So I go into the field to drive them out, I'm riding the quad bike. Instantly half of them follow me because I might have food (I told you they were being pampered) and the other half stand and watch because they don't think I've got food so aren't going to waste time following me. But be damned if they're going to miss out if suddenly food appears.

So I'm trying to follow the ewes who're following me and at the same time not upset anybody and also get them to move as a group out through the gate.

So eventually they all turn round and move out of the gate. They have to go the correct way down the lane, because of the gate. But across the lane is a fence. Someone had to take a digger through the hedge and there's a fence of hurdles across the gap. It's fine, it's kept sheep in place for months. No problems.

Except this morning these heavily pregnant ewes who're not supposed to get too excited hit this fence of hurdles like the tide and just poured over it, flattening it. Shouting the distinctive vernacular phrase "Ya bluidy auld witch" I'm left in the other field watching the chaos develop. So I had to shut the gate behind me, re-arrange the hurdles and get the sheep out of this field and back onto the lane.

Of course at this point some of them started following me again. I suppose you could see their point. Perhaps it was this field that I was going to feed them in. From the sheep point of view this adequately explained why I hadn't fed them in the previous field. The fact it was them who'd smashed down the fence so they were in this field passed them by entirely. Cattle know when they're 'escaped' or are in the wrong place, and can get all excited or guilty about it. Sheep have no concept of having escaped. They're just where they are.

So I finally got them moving again, back into the original field that they'd first escaped from. At this point they discovered the food that was waiting for them. A feeder full of silage and a bucket of molasses (when we pamper, we pamper) and they immediately piled round these and started eating. Occasionally stopping to look at me with the sort of expression which said, "About time as well."

The fact that they'd abandoned both silage and molasses to go ratching about in strange fields was apparently my fault. But anyway I spent the rest of the morning before the rain hit fixing things they'd damaged in transit. This meant that it wasn't until dinnertime that I had a chance once more to turn to creating deathless prose.

Admittedly today fine literature and tackling the eternal verities will probably amount to an article on rural fuel poverty but we cannot have everything.

Ya bluidy auld witch

It's a phrase I'd never come across until I started working with sheep. It's normally directed at the misbegotten mule ewe who wiggles, burrows and climbs through or under netting, snapping off posts and generally creating a gap which the rest come pouring through.

From experience the Mule (normally round here a cross between Blue faced Leicester and Swaledale) is the worst culprit. They're the normal 'breeding sheep', the mothers of this year's lambs. They have the toughness and mothering ability of their own Swaledale mothers, and because their mothers are fell sheep, they're prone to wandering.
Down breeds aren't such a problem, and they provide the sires of this year's lambs, because they've better confirmation, grow faster and taste better. But they're not as hardy and aren't such determinedly good mothers.
And we've fetched a batch home because they're coming up to lamb. In another month the first of them will have lambed and things will be hectic. So we fetch them home, pamper them a bit, make sure they properly fed and generally treat them as you'd expect expectant mothers to be treated.
But their condition doesn't stop the bluidy auld witches 'ratching' through every fence looking for better grazing. The problem is, there is one field with a little bit of grass. We've been saving it for them, so they can go on it after they've lambed.
But of course they've found it now, and they just keep breaking fences down to get to it. And of course I just keep putting the fences back up again, strengthening the weak spots and generally trying to make sure the fence is as stock proof as I can. But it's a fair length of fence and bits that appeared OK yesterday were the ones they went through last night.
So after I've posted this I'm back out to have another go. There are things I should be doing; after all they're robbing the world of my deathless prose. (Or alternatively saving folk from having to read my petty scribblings.)

Blow your nose in your handkerchief.

You know what it is, one of those occasions when you're not sure whether you want to laugh or just disappear quietly and hope everybody else is too embarrassed by their part in the events ever to mention them again.
But it was really just one of those things. I'd be about fifteen and like pretty well every farmer's son (or at least livestock farmer's son) when not at school I tended to help out a fair bit. Indeed there were various jobs which were planned around school holidays.
But one job everybody ends up doing is standing in junctions making sure that livestock turn in the right direction. So it was no surprise that at about 4pm one Saturday afternoon I was standing in the lane at the top of our drive turning dairy cows into the yard as they walked down the road.
What was a surprise was that at this point, the headmaster of the school I attended should walk down the lane with his wife and daughter. Now Fred Robinson might not have been the best headmaster in the world. I genuinely wouldn't know, I never worked for him. But one thing he did was he made sure he knew every boy in his school. In the first year (we had 90 boys a year come into the school and they were divided into three classes) he taught one class Biology, one class Chemistry (because they're what he taught before his elevation to the pinnacle of absolute power) and the third class he taught Religious Education. So at the end of the year he knew every boy in that year.
All this meant for me on this occasion was that there was no way I could feign ignorance of who he was. Also in spite of my jeans, torn shirt and battered baseball cap (the perfect accessories for dirty wellies) he was going to recognise me.
So he said 'Good afternoon' and I explained why it wasn't wise to proceed, due to a herd of dairy cows somnolently meandering down the road towards us and he and his two companions stood next to me to watch the spectacle.

Now cows are inherently curious. They will walk up to people who appear non-threatening. They will sniff them, they will even try and curl their tongue round the edge of a garment and pull it into their mouth whilst they chew it, meditatively. Anyway half a dozen stopped to look at these people I had with me and one walked that step further, stuck its neck out and lowered its head to sniff the headmaster.

Now there's no point sniffing something if your nose is blocked, is it? So it snorted out what seemed like a pint of the stuff all over his coat.

I kept my eyes firmly forward and made sure I didn't see it. The rest of the cows came along as did my father, accompanied, for the purpose of training, by Lassie, our young Border Collie. She wasn't really old enough to work, but was a bit more than a pup. But she could learn her trade walking behind dairy cows. Now Border Collies can be a bit standoffish. I've been told it's because they have a small natural 'pack' size, and anyone not in the 'pack' (which is basically just the family they live with) is to be regarded as hostile or at least a damned nuisance.

But when they're young, especially when they're on farms and don't see many people anyway, strange people are an exciting novelty. So Lassie bounded over towards this group of strange people. Now it has to be admitted that I was probably too traumatised by what had happened previously to realise what was going to happen next. Young Border Collies like their ears tickling, they like to talk to you, to look you in the eyes and be friends. But they're not what you'd call a big dog. So they achieve this by jumping up and placing their front feet on an appropriate part of your anatomy. The fact that Lassie hadn't wiped her feet after following sixty milk cows down a muddy lane explains the state of her feet, and the muddy footprints she left on the trouser suit of the Headmaster's daughter.

My father restored order with the words "Siddown ya bluidy dog," and she trotted back to look after the cows. I made my excuses and left.

Obviously I am on the road to recovery from this experience. However I'm self-funding the counselling by selling my novels at a reasonable price. If your conscience has been troubled by this story then you can help by purchasing one of these books.

Chuffed to bits I was.

Every so often good things happen at random
So there I was. Every couple of hours, if nobody competent is about, I have to walk through the three lambing sheds to check nothing is happening. The ladies are pretty slow at the moment, so at some point everything is going to happen at once and we'll be swamped. But at the moment we've got a couple of ewes lambing a day. This isn't a lot when 400 have to lamb by the start of April.
Anyway I was walking down one shed and a ewe had just dropped a lamb. Great, open a pen gate, whisk her and her lamb into the pen.
Now according to her mark she'd been scanned for a single. So at this point it's worth trying to 'wet mother' another lamb onto her so she's got two.
So I go into the other shed where the triplets are and borrow a 'spare lamb' from one of them.
This is because a ewe has two teats so really can only feed two lambs properly, so a third lamb tends to be fostered onto a ewe who only has one.
I collect a lamb, who isn't entirely impressed by the fuss, and a disposable plastic glove. This is because the lamb is about to be drenched in afterbirth and similar so it smells like its new mother.

Everything prepared I walk back into the first shed, and as I'm about to climb into the pen, I notice that the lady in question has just dropped a second lamb and is contentedly licking that one down as well.
So the 'spare lamb' goes back to mum for a little while and I get on with the rest of the day, whistling cheerfully.
It's funny how such little things do make your day isn't it.

Sheep, a socket set and a dog that howls back at police cars.

For simple country folk we lead complicated lives. It started when I let the dog out. Or perhaps it really started when the wheel bearing went on the quad trailer? But anyway, it was obvious the bearing was going so there was a replacement bearing sitting, pristine and jewel like in its wrapping.
Before I could get hay to sheep I needed the trailer and before I could use the trailer I would need to change the wheel bearing. And Sal, the dog, was getting bored and wanted out. So I let her out and started on the wheel bearing.
Now I like to take the wheel off first. Then I can put the hub in a bucket of hot water and detergent and clean it. So that way I know what's happening. And then obviously it makes sense to clean off the axle as well. But as I'm doing this, I glance up and notice Sal walking backwards and looking distinctly unhappy.
Now it occurs to me that some explanation is called for. We're lambing at the moment and the minute Sal is let out in a morning, she goes straight to the lambing shed.

Not only is there the off chance of a bit of afterbirth, but joy of joys, there might be a bit of skin. Because sometimes if a lamb dies you skin it, put the skin on an orphan so the mother assumes that it's the same lamb. That way she'll let it suckle, and once it's successfully suckled for a couple of days it smells like its new mum anyway and you can take the extra skin off.

From the point of view of a Border Collie, this is dog-chew heaven!

But if you remember an earlier blog, a common term used to describe mule ewes is 'ya bluidy auld witch'. Apparently this isn't a dialect term, as it is used by shepherds from Somerset to Shap.

And this morning, one bluidy auld witch had got out of her lambing pen, and with her two lambs in tow, was taking the morning air. I don't think she had any set destination in mind, other than 'out'.

So as she came out of the shed in one direction, she met Sal going into the shed in the other direction. Now normally this would have had one result, the ewe would have retreated back into the shed. But this ewe had two lambs. Now the maternal instinct can be strong in sheep. It seems to vary between individuals, and it's something that has been bred for over the years. Indeed when 'mothering on', or trying to fit the third lamb from a set of triplets onto a ewe who only had a single, you depend heavily on this maternal instinct to kick in.

Indeed our previous dog, Jess, was encouraged to drift round the lambing shed on the grounds that her presence could arouse the protective maternal instinct in a tup!

So Sal, a dog so open and helpful that she howls back at the sirens on emergency vehicles, had run into a ewe, tooled up with lord alone knows how many millennia of selective breeding for maternal instinct.

At this point we had a communications breakdown. Thinking about it, probably a three species communication breakdown.

I just wanted them to sort themselves out so I could change the bearing. Sal was just interested in anything she might find to nibble on. The ewe had taken one look at Sal's teeth, a silhouette which doubtless matched perfectly the one marked 'wolf' in 'A sheep's guide to the predators of the world' and suspected that this nibbling might involve her lambs.
So she stamped her foot.
Other species can be more spectacularly demonstrative. The roar of the lion, the snarl of big dog; they're all pretty graphic warnings.
A sheep has a bleat that never sounds less than plaintive, and dentition that threatens nobody. So they stamp a front foot.
From the human point of view this doesn't work well. It places them very firmly into 'petulant infant' territory. What you must remember is that sheep have one good attack. Head down and hell for leather at whoever is the problem. It works best with bigger targets like people. Dogs are a bit nippy and unless the sheep can get the dog in a corner, the dog will probably escape.
But Sal wasn't looking for trouble. She was walking backwards looking nervous and the ewe, her two lambs clustering round her, had a triumphal gleam in her eye. Unfortunately I didn't have time for all this. A hot date with a socket set and a wheel bearing called, and after that I had work to do. So I just walked past the dog and up to the ewe. Who stamped her foot!
At which point I called her a bluidy auld witch and told her to get back in the shed. This she did, her lambs leading the way as she kept turning and looking past me to keep an eye on the dog. Sal just slunk about looking embarrassed. So I tied the hurdle back up and got on with the bearing.

Hanging on in there

Now personally I don't believe in letting sheep have Facebook accounts and a presence on social media, but there are times when you read some posts and you being to suspect that others are not of this opinion and have set up the accounts for their domesticated animals, such is the wit, erudition and grasp of basic grammar that they display.

But it has to be said that we've half a dozen ladies who, at the moment, might as well be spending their time on Facebook.

Part way through pregnancy, all the ewes were scanned, and then split up into groups depending on how many lambs they were carrying. Those carrying three need especially pampering and so pampering they got.

When they were eventually brought in to lamb they were put in one shed with plenty of bedding and 'left to get on with it.'

Most did. So much so that the individual pens in the shed are now used to house other ewes who've lambed elsewhere and can take time to properly bond with their lambs and come to their full milk production.

The last six due to give birth to triplets watch this process with benign contempt and slouch about in comfort, looking heavier and heavier.

Now once they lamb, they'll have a couple of days in an individual pen and then they'll be out into a field with their lambs to get on with life. After all, outside is their environment and they're supposed to be happier there.

But what with all this global warming and climate change and whatever, this March has been as miserable as any we've had recently. And these six ladies have peered through the bars of the gate, weighed the job in the balance, and have obviously decided that, do you know what? Inside, on straw, with someone bringing a lunch tray round a couple of times a day, and silage there should you fancy a nibble between meals, seems a better option.

So far it's been well over a week since anybody lambed in that building. In the others, mothers are popping lambs out and leading them out heroically into the bright new world. But these six, legs firmly crossed, seem to be hanging on for better weather, warm spring breezes and the promise of new grass.

Ode to the auld white faced witch with her head stuck in the dike

There was something I was going to tell you, but blowed if I can remember. But anyway, for those who're following matters of ovine importance, one of the six ladies with their legs crossed waiting for spring has finally decided to lamb. She had two large twin lambs rather than the triplets she was scanned for, but even she couldn't have coped with three lambs the size of these two.

But anyway we had a real Luke 15:4 moment yesterday. We'd stuck four ewes and their lambs on the lawn. (Yes, our lawn is fenced for sheep.) It's an intermediate destination for those ewes and their lambs who aren't quite 100% but really ought to be outside.

Except that one ratching auld witch wiggled her way through the dike and the others followed her. Anyway we found them and fetched them home. All bar for one lamb who seemed to have got lost.

So whilst I put thorns in the gap, people went to look for the lamb but still no sign. Finally I took Sal and walked along the route the ewes had taken. At one point I heard a bleat. By the time I heard the second bleat Sal was hurtling at about mach three in the direction of the bleat. When I arrived on the scene Sal was dancing round the lamb who was looking a little put out by the performance.

So I caught the lamb. In this case I didn't "lay it on my shoulders, rejoicing" because frankly the poor little mite wasn't big enough. It tucked nicely under my arm whilst Sal trotted behind with the professionally 'keen' expression worn by Border Collies who've achieved something.

This morning on the other hand she was less successful. I was feeding hay to one lot of ewes and noticed one was staying by the fence. I drove across on the quad and discovered that, yes; the white faced auld witch had been pushing through and had got her head stuck in the netting. Unfortunately her way of resolving this was to keep pushing forwards. Sal was entirely in agreement with this approach and the two of them seemed to be working on the principle that if the head got through, the body will follow. I confess at this point I was forced to remonstrate with both of them; indeed I may even have descended to vulgar abuse.

But eventually, after a frank and open exchange of views, I managed to get her head out and she trotted off to join her lambs and then glared at me in a most affronted manner.

We are not the men our grandfathers were

They say that behind every good software writer there is a man with a mallet to tell him when to stop.

Fixing fences is a bit like that. It's normally comparatively easy to know where to start, but working out when you've got the fence 'good enough' as opposed to 'good' is a more subjective decision.

The problem is I remember what it was like in my grandfather's day. I was only a kid, but I saw, and worked under, the old regime. On a weekend when I wasn't at school, I've thinned turnips by hand and planted potatoes by hand as well. By the time I was at senior school my grandfather had retired and we'd given up on turnips and potatoes and gone over to livestock.

In the way that these things can happen, for a number of years I farmed exactly the same land as my grandfather did. He had thirty-two dairy cows, plus 'followers'. That probably means he had another forty or fifty younger cattle. He also had sixty sheep. Then he'd grow a few acres of barley for feed, a few acres of turnips or kale, and a couple of acres of potatoes.

He worked himself, employed two or three full time men and a 'lad'. Financially he 'did alright', had holidays most years and a prosperous retirement.

On the same land, at one point I had seventy dairy cows plus thirty sucklers and over a hundred young stock. This I farmed with one full time man. We got to the stage that we realised the full time man was the only person getting a living out of the place and we re-jigged the business so I was working on my own rearing up to 240 young stock a year, buying them as calves and selling them at between a year and two years old.

But during this time I also had to work as a freelance journalist/writer to ensure we did have an income every year.

For the next generation, those who're doing most of the work now, the job is even harder. On the same land there are over 400 ewes and an indeterminate number of cattle (their number depends on price and cash flow).

But as well as this, you've got to work six or seven hours a day somewhere else to make a living.

So there's me, fixing a fence. It was fine when I started, but eventually it started to drizzle. Not enough to be worth going back home for a coat, so I just kept going.

Now remember my idea of what a hedge and fence should look like was determined when this farm had four adult men and a lad working full time. That's the sort of workforce that created and maintained the countryside people claim to love.

I finally decided that the fence was 'good enough' at about the same time that it stopped being drizzle and became torrential rain with added sleet for seasonal variety.

And what will happen to the countryside? Who knows? Government claims to put money into it with environmental payments. The amounts are derisory. Certainly they're not enough to employ the three extra men that this farm used to have and it's the labour of these men that kept everything maintained properly. Last time I checked, even if we could get the environmental payments, we'd get the princely sum of about £3,000 a year. I'd struggle to employ two men and a lad on that.

But money has been bled out of the industry. As a general rule of thumb you can reckon that each generation can live entirely on organic food and only spend the same proportion of their income on food as their parents did, buying conventional food.

So where's the money gone? Think what you spend money on now that you didn't spend it on before. I saw one comment that most families in the UK spend more a week on their Sky subscription than they do on meat. Similarly, the money for the mobile phone contract, thirty years ago there wasn't even the concept of one of them, what has society stopped spending on to pay for that? Or TV boxed sets? Is money being spent on them rather than books, or beer in pubs or on buying decent food or what?

My guess is that we'll get more and more posturing. People might even vote 'Green'. But what has gone has gone. The countryside is changing and will continue to change; we'll lose stuff because people don't really want it as much as they want the other stuff.

And me, I'll keep plodding on, remembering how it should be done because I'm old enough to have seen it done properly.

Tek care, lambs ont road.

I was going to call this piece "dogging", because that's what it's about but I decided to approach things from a somewhat different angle.

Way back I remember somebody writing that they were walking in the countryside and could see in the distance somebody ploughing. As they walked along the path that ran beside the field they obviously fell into some romantic daydream about honest sons of the soil working in their own rural idyll, cut off from the pressures and hurly burly of the twentieth (as it was then) century.
Except that as they got to where the tractor was turning on the headland they could hear Radio 2 coming from the tractor radio. They suddenly realised just how pervasive and all embracing modern culture is.
It's the same with the sign, 'Tek care, Lambs ont road' that you occasionally see in Cumbria. Because of the need to have broadband to run a business, and the fact that coverage extends out even into some rural areas, Facebook and suchlike have penetrated even into the depths of darkest rurality.
Facebook memes and pictures of cute cats are as likely to be familiar in hidden villages as they are in Central London. Thus it might be impossible for a Cumbrian sheep-farmer to write a sign which says "Lambs on the road, please take care." At the very least a sense of ironic post modernism would drive him to use the more 'traditional' message.
This of course leads us to ask what the lambs are doing on the road in the first place. Well it boils down to two facts, lambs are small and they are inquisitive. So when they're not hungry they'll wander about poking their noses into things. This means they can unwittingly creep through gaps that aren't really there. Suddenly they're not in the field, they're on the road, and mum isn't in sight and they're starting to feel peckish. At this point there's a lot of frantic bleating as they try and work out where mum is and pick the shortest practical route to her.
Now it sometimes happens that people wander along and find a lamb asleep or in the wrong place, without its mother. I've known them pick the lamb up, carry it miles to the nearest farm and hand it to the farmer because they feel it obviously needs looking after.

But unless the lamb is physically trapped, or ostentatiously injured, it almost certainly doesn't. If you leave it there, at some point mum will wander over, or the lamb will feel peckish and wander back to mum. By moving it all that happens is that the lamb now smells of you. When you give it to the farmer it then starts smelling of him, and even if he can find the mother, the mother is going to be a bit suspicious of this strange smelling creature that he's presenting her with.

That being said (for those of you who're wondering when I'm going to start writing about dogging) there can be times when you do have to move ewes and lambs and the lambs can be a nightmare if they get themselves turned round and suddenly cannot find mum. At which point they'll set off at speed in the direction they think mum ought to be.

From my experience yesterday a lamb can run at about 16mph. I cannot. However on the quad (which has a speedometer so I have a fair idea of the speed everything was moving at) I can keep up with the little beggar. That being said it has a turning circle a lot tighter than mine. But this is where your dog comes in. Sal, our Border Collie bitch, seems to be able to run at 27mph, at least for a short while. She can do 16mph while looking back over her shoulder to see if I'm following. (To be fair she really shouldn't. The time when she inadvertently ran into a middle aged and utterly respectable ewe was an embarrassment to both dog and sheep.) Her turning circle is also on a par with the lambs.

Hence as the lamb sets off for the further horizon, moving at least 16mph, both dog and I set off after it. And this is where the 'dogging' starts because Sal will dog the lamb, keeping up with it, trying to turn it back to me or at least trap it in a corner where I can finally catch it.

It's something of a battle of wits between the two animals as the lamb isn't as afraid of the dog as you might think and will happily try and nip behind it or jump over it or generally out manoeuvre it. Still we finally caught the little beggar and with it under one arm we went to catch up with the rest of them, moved them all through the gate, put the lamb back with the flock and left them to it.

Feeling sheepish?

So, we've three-hundred and ninety something lambed, and five left to lamb. They could spin it out over the next three or four weeks so there isn't the sense of driving urgency.
But what about the rest? What happens to those who have lambed? Let us assume that we take the standard 'set' of one ewe with her twin lambs. They don't go out until we're happy that mum recognised her lambs (and lambs recognise mum) and she's feeding them properly. Once we're happy with that they go out into a field with other sheep.
At this point we have to be a bit particular. We try to put them out with ewes who have lambs of the same age, so they settle down well together. We also try to put them out into a field with not many other ewes and lambs into it. So they go out in batches of about twenty five. To anthropomorphise wildly, think about taking your toddler to school for the first time. You'll be happier to let them join a class of twenty to thirty, all of the same age, than a class of five hundred which includes everything up to and including eighteen year olds.
And it's at this point that things start getting complicated. Lambs have nothing to do with their time other than eat and explore. They squeeze through gaps and wander off, with mum bleating pathetically behind them.

You can end up with the lamb in one field, wandering round the strange ewes, all with their own lambs, trying to work out which is mum, whilst mum is in the other field wondering where little one has gone to.
Trying to do anything about this is tricky. Evolution decided that lambs needed speed with a side order of curiosity and a dash of 'cuteness'. Intellect wasn't regarded as a survival characteristic. So when you try to catch the lamb to put it back it can pull moves that would make a Parkour champion applaud. Although to be fair you get the feeling that the lamb concentrates on the jump, gets the leap right, and only worries about landing as it travels through the air. They don't tend to plan their moves out in advance.
This lack of sparkling intellect is also shared by mum. She might have two lambs but isn't good on advanced maths and if she decides to travel, so long as at least one of them is tagging along behind her, she feels reasonably happy.
You find that those who lose their mum, either by misplacing her or because she's ill, tend to pinch milk off other mums when they get a chance. By the time they're about six weeks old, they're old enough to cope with solid food alone and they tend to wander more, coming back for a free feed and to get their washing done.
Illness is a difficult one. Sheep aren't domesticated in the way that even cats are. They are far less domesticated than cattle. So they don't just come and watch you, or stand and let you watch them in the same way that you can with cattle. Also there is an issue with herd animals. Evolution has designed them not to show weakness. The weak one is the one the predator picks, so both cattle and sheep can carry illnesses and even injuries and look remarkably healthy. It takes a lot of skill to spot illness in its early stages. So at the moment life consists of a lot of careful sheep watching, trying to spot trouble before it gets too far out of hand.
There are times when you ponder whether life should be so sheep centred. So it's nice when you can do things that don't include sheep in any way, shape or form.

Lambing

I just thought I'd sort of describe 'lambing' for people. I know there's 'Lambing Live' on telly (or was, I haven't a clue whether they're doing it this year or not) but I thought people would like a peep behind the curtain.

Lambing 'starts' when you put the tups in. (Tups is the Cumbrian term for rams, male sheep). This year we were cunning, we split the ewes into two groups, each of two hundred. We put the tups into one group, so they'd start lambing in the middle of February, and then three weeks later we put the tups into the next group as well. The idea was that lambing would be spread out a little bit and wouldn't get totally manic. By and large it worked.

Round about Christmas we had sheep scanned. This told us who was carrying a single, twins or triplets. They were split into groups because they'd all need different diets.

The middle of February arrived. Prior to that we'd been taking hay and silage out to the ewes in the fields, and those carrying triplets had been really pampered getting ewe rolls. All got molasses as well because they really need the energy.

Then as the first ewes started lambing we went through them, pulled out those who were nearest to lambing and brought them inside. We have three old cattle sheds and we just bed them with straw, but along the sides we have some individual pens made out of hurdles. When things were busy somebody would go through every hour or so and if a ewe was lambing or had just lambed you'd quietly escort her into one of the pens and let her lick her lambs down in peace and generally give her a chance to get to know them.

One problem you can have during lambing is when you find three ewes surrounded by anywhere from five to seven lambs, and nobody (including the mothers,) has the faintest idea who belongs to who! So whisking them off to their private maternity suite as soon as you spot them doing anything saves problems.

There are other issues, large lambs that need help out into the world, lambs coming backwards, lambs lying across the birth canal they're supposed to be going down, but most ewes manage this sort of thing entirely on their own. After all why not, it's a perfectly natural process; the species has been doing it for millennia.

Once the ewe has lambed she and her lambs are whisked into another building, again in individual pens, where she can bond properly with the lambs and we can check that she's got the milk to feed them. If she's the mother of triplets then she cannot really feed three adequately so one is quietly removed. Ideally it goes straight onto a ewe who has only had one lamb. In the perfect world you catch the ewe with a single lamb as she is giving birth. That means you can rub a 'spare' lamb down in afterbirth and fluid so the doting mum takes it as her own. (This is what we call round here Wet adoption.) Otherwise you can go through up to three stages. Some, a very few, will just accept the extra lamb. Some you put a halter on so that they cannot drive the lamb off, and so eventually, after a couple of days it smells of them and they accept it. Some have to go into a formal lamb adopter where the ewe's head is held and she cannot see the lambs at all. So she forgets which is which and they both smell like her. But with this system, once she has accepted the lamb you're best putting the new happy family into a single pen so that the lambs learn to recognise Mum's face.

But across the board, once you know Mum has accepted the lambs, and each lamb has a nice full tummy which shows that she's feeding them properly; then they can go back outside.

And this is where the weather is crucial. We've got fertiliser on, grass should be growing but because it's cold and wet we're feeding them as much silage and hay as we were back in January. There just isn't enough grass yet to allow the ewes to produce enough milk to support their lambs. Obviously they're also still getting their ewe rolls to make sure they are getting enough quality food so they can feed their lambs.

Ideally, the sun comes out, the mixture of rain, sleet and snow stops, and the grass starts growing. As the grass grows we can slowly withdraw the extra feed until finally Mum is feeding her lambs solely off the grass, and the lambs are also eating grass as well.

As you can imagine, things get hectic. You have anywhere between a month and six weeks flat out. Our busiest day saw fifteen lamb within twenty four hours. That is quite civilised and a result of us spreading tupping. But ideally you don't plan to do anything else much during lambing. Social events are just not booked for then and friends have to accept that you might just disappear for a month.

You certainly don't plan a book launch for the middle of it like this idiot did!

To get there I wouldn't start from here

All my life I've lived at a place accessible only by travelling down a narrow lane. But because our lane meets the main road at both ends, we do get passing traffic. Not a lot because intelligent people know that if you're in a hurry, a single track road is not going to be a reliable short cut. Over the years we've had many interesting or even amusing moments because of it. Like for example the time my mother was pretty seriously unwell. She was sitting in the front room, looking out over the road, and a couple of her sisters came to visit. They were sitting chatting and suddenly my mother went quiet and was staring at the road. They wondered if her meds had just kicked in. Indeed my mother wondered if her meds had just kicked in, because she could see a bus driving past our gate. Fortunately her sisters turned in time, saw the bus, and she had witnesses to support her claim. But we reckon it's the first bus in at least seventy years. We still haven't a clue what it was doing there.

Another game we used to play when silaging was 'how many cars did you get to reverse.' The thing about carting silage is that you're pulling a trailer that pretty well blocks visibility. Now being a competent tractor driver you can reverse it. You can see the hedges on both sides and with care and not rushing you can quietly back down the lane. What you cannot see is anything in the lane. So you don't back a silage trailer in the lane without somebody acting as a 'banksman' to ensure that there isn't a car, a motorbike, a mum with a pram or a lass on a pony, trapped in the lane behind you.

So when you're carting silage down the lane and meet a car, the car driver has two options. They can reverse out of your way, or they can stop the car. Get out, help you reverse, walk back to their car and drive on.

So the person carting would normally get back to the pit and say to the person with the buckrake, 'Two,' or even 'Three'. This was the number of cars that had had to reverse that trip.

Eventually I did the equivalent of getting a maximum break in Snooker. We used to get a lot of the 'eleven car treasure hunts.' From memory I think the rule was that if you had less than twelve cars involved in an event, you didn't need to inform the police when you were organising it. The good ones were genuine treasure hunts, follow the clues, do some thinking, work out where to go next. The bad ones were just ad hoc rallies where you got the excuse to tear round narrow lanes at dangerously high speeds. On this occasion, as I drove down the lane, I found myself facing all eleven cars coming the other way. There was no way I could reverse so all eleven had to. But what really made my day was the lad in the eleventh car. He'd got this battered old banger; everybody else was driving reasonably smart cars. He backed his into a gate way, let the other ten back past him and as I drove past him I got a big grin and a thumbs up from him and his girlfriend as they pulled back out into the lane and set off to exploit their unexpected lead.

The other ten were less enthused.

The other thing that can happen is that the main road gets blocked. At this point some clown almost inevitably diverts traffic down our lane. It might not matter too much if they only diverted them down in one direction, but when they send them down in two directions it's madness. On one occasion the postman was caught in the chaos and it took him an hour and a half to get out.

It happened again last week. Somebody knocked on our door. They were local and knew me and asked if we could put cars in our yard to get them off the lane. We did, watched the queue snake past, and then unleashed the contents of the yard into the lane, only for them to meet the next queue forty yards further on.

We did what we normally do in these circumstances. Phone the police and ask them to block one end.

But even when they do this, it can still be stimulating. A few years back now we were fetching cows home to milk and oldest daughter stood in the lane to turn the cows down towards home as the dog and I brought them out of the field. As the dog and I were doing this a queue of cars was building up and I could hear somebody in the queue shouting and blowing their horn.

Anyway there wasn't anything I could do about it, so we just quietly got all the cows out onto the lane and they walked placidly towards home, ignoring shouting and horn blowing idiots. I closed the gate after them, stepped out into the road and suddenly there was total silence.

Amazing the number of people who'll insult a young lass but shut up when her dad appears isn't it.

Working for the bank?

Somehow bank holidays have always rather passed me by. Being self-employed all my life they were an irrelevance and when I employed people they were a damned nuisance.

I remember one morning getting into the house after finally finishing morning milking. Because of electrical problems I'd managed to finish milking by the simple expedient of running extension leads over the roof and plugging stuff into them. But before I finally got my breakfast I thought I'd phone the electrician.

The conversation went something like this.

"Hi Colin, Jim Webster here."

A somewhat sleepy voice said, "Jim do you know what day it is?"

After a brief pause to check I replied with reasonable confidence, "Monday."

"It's a bank holiday."

"Didn't know you worked for a bank Colin."

Colin being Colin, he came out and after an hour he'd got whatever it was fixed and I wasn't relying on extension leads in the rain.

As it is, because today's been fine I've got quite a few jobs finished off. Two fences fixed where a couple of old ewes have managed to jump over or squeeze through, and another fence that I put up in the rain on Saturday, finished off in the dry today.

That and a quad trailer gate fixed and bits and bobs of other stuff and it's not been a bad day.

But what is the point of going anywhere on a bank holiday? The roads are always busy, everywhere you might fancy going is busy, and a lot of stuff will be shut as well. Or if it isn't they're shorthanded because who in their right mind pays staff double for working bank holidays?

Effectively the great and the good have decided that the British Public WILL celebrate whatever it is (be it Labour Day, or New Years Day). Why not just add it to their days off so they can take it when they want?

Give everybody the right to certain days as holiday if they wanted, out of their holiday entitlement. So if for religious reasons you wanted to take off Good Friday, Christmas Day and Ascension Day (or the beginning and end of Ramadan or whatever) you could and your employer just had to put up with it.

Given that apparently the banks are starting to open on 'Bank Holidays' at the very least they're going to have to change the name.

Mind you, at one point it did irritate me. Having run a business when interest rates on overdrafts were over 20% I felt that I was working for the bank, because they were the only ones making any money. Yet I was the one who wasn't getting the bank holidays

Ah, the good old days. One of the best days of my life was when I finally got clear of the bank and no longer owed them a penny.

The perfect body.

Ah, but the problems of body image. In spite of all the advertising by organisations like Chanel, Dolce & Gabbana, Gucci, Loxottica, Versace, or Yves Saint Laurent, what sticks in mind is a comment made to me by an old farmer looking at a pen of bullocks. "If it's got a backside like your mother and shoulders like your father, it's doing alright." But we were shearing sheep the other day. Sheep have been wearing the same jacket since last June. Some of them are starting to look a bit ragged around the edges. Others still have a full firm fleece and look like a big solid sheep.

So buggerlugs here pushes them into the race. This leads up onto the shearing trailer where two lads, younger and fitter than me, are doing the actual shearing.

If you get it right, some nearly knock you out of the way in their haste to keep up with the rest of them, running up the ramp without me having anything to do with it. Others dig their feet in and have to be pushed up.

And then they meet the shearer. Up until this point they're almost defined by their fleece, at least to a non-shepherd like me. The amount of wool, the way it hangs, the gaps, the smit marks, produce an image which might just mean I can recognise the animal.

Then, a short while later, sheared, the animal leaps down off the trailer, a lighter and somewhat different animal. Some of them are revealed to be big, thickset ewes, solid, even plump. Others are less well built, some are even scrawny. At this stage in the proceedings I suspect even the lambs are a bit nonplussed by it all and check first before making any assumptions as to just who is Mum. And as we're taking them back out into the field, the scrawny one at the back stops to check that it still has two lambs. And the shepherd points to her and says, "Bluidy good ewe that. Two damned good lambs every year and she rears them well."

Of maggots, sheep, and summer wellies

You know what it's like. I had a busy day ahead of me. Work to do, people to contact, the internet to spam unmercifully in the hope that I'd sweet talk somebody into buying my chuffing book.

So it's off to a good start. Straight after breakfast I go to check the sheep and see that everything's OK and where it should be.

Anyway I was walking through the gimmer lambs and one caught my eye. It was somehow looking a bit grubby and dejected. I tried to get closer but it wasn't having that. It accelerated away, so obviously wasn't too ill. But I wasn't happy with it.

At this time of the year we can have problems with blowfly attacking sheep. If the wool is dirty or matted the blowfly lay their eggs in it and then the maggots quite literally eat the sheep alive. I was going to include a photo of this but good taste and a fear that you might have just eaten stopped me.

It's one of the reasons we dip sheep. The problem with dipping sheep is that we have to use organophosphate because nothing else has been developed that works and isn't even more dangerous. So you try to get away without dipping, or at least keep on top of problems so you only have to dip them only once.

This is because the chemical stays in their fleece and gives them protection from blowflies and similar for some weeks. Obviously you cannot kill them for human consumption during this period.

But anyway I decided that after checking all the other batches I'd come back and fetch this batch home and pull out the one I was worried about and treat it. When I got home I got all the gates ready, got on the quad and set off to get them. To be fair, they cooperated reasonably. The first problem was one gimmer who just sat down and lay there. I checked her feet. She'd got maggots eating into them. So I picked her up, put her on the back of the quad and set off to keep the others moving. At this point I noticed that a growing number of them were building up on the bank of the beck. The beck was dug out fifty years ago. It looks more like an anti-tank ditch with a small canal at the bottom than some rippling mountain stream. The gimmers were obviously planning to surge across in a bunch. I left the one on the back of the quad behind and shot off to discourage them. They saw me coming and scattered back into the field and eventually noticed the bridge and started crossing it.

I went back for the lame lamb and followed. As I trailed along behind the last one across the bridge I could hear bleating below me. One of the idiots had gone into the beck rather than over the bridge. Immediately I ran through the triage. It had got itself stuck on a mass of weed; it wasn't going anywhere and would struggle to drown in ten minutes. So I left it, drove most of the rest before me, (some had cut off to the right to graze) and got home. Here I put the lame lamb in a pen to treat later, grabbed my crook and set off back to the beck.

Now the crook was designed with this beck in mind. Far too often a sheep will fall in the beck. You go down the bank to help her out, and she just goes to the far side of the beck. You walk 200 yards to the bridge, cross the beck and walk 200 yards back. You go down the bank to help her out and she crosses to the far side again. My crook is over twelve feet long and was made from round steel bar. I can stand on either bank and catch them and pull them out. Neighbours turn up to borrow it occasionally!

But anyway it's not the handiest thing to carry on a quad bike, but there's a job to be done and I'm the only one about to do it. So I arrive at the beck. First I use the crook to tear away some of the weed to create a channel, then using the crook I pull the lamb down the channel towards me. I catch it and drag it out onto the bank.

At this point note that the lamb will weigh 30kg or thereabouts. It'll have another 10kg of water in its fleece, perhaps 20kg. Discussing pulling it out is far easier than doing it. But still it was out and I got it back to the others. Anyway I collected the bunch that had been grazing and took them back. I specifically noted that the grubby looking one that I'd been concerned about was with them. I rounded them up, they split to go both sides of a clump of trees and I followed one bunch and went back for the others. Gathered together again I brought them home but realised that somewhere the grubby one had disappeared. So I went back, hunted and couldn't find it.

I went back again, this time with Sal, on the grounds that her nose is better than mine and she covers the ground faster.

Well it's a good theory, but in reality there was me walking through the clumps of rushes, whilst Sal, who is not a tall dog as Border Collies go, was bouncing about trying to see over the rushes.

But anyway we came to a gutter. It's got a hedge growing on both sides and I'd walked the length of it before, looking, but this time Sal found the lamb. It hadn't merely fallen in the water and got stuck in the never-ending glutinous mud that makes up the bottom. It had managed to work its way out of sight to do this. But obviously not out of Border Collie sight or scent.

Now I knew where it was.

So if I grabbed this branch with my left hand and swung out and put my right foot just there where the bank might just hold me, I should be able to grab the lamb.

So I did. And it worked. Great.

Unfortunately as I pulled on the lamb, I was bracing myself with my right foot and the bank slowly crumbled and my foot slid gracefully into the water. And the more I pulled, the deep my foot went.

At this point I feel I ought to introduce you to the concept of 'Summer Wellies.' In winter it's raining, it's wet, there is water everywhere and you wear wellies all the time to keep your feet dry.

But wellies wear out. In my case they almost always split at the level of my Achilles tendon, where I press my foot to grip the other welly when I'm taking it off.

In the case of my right welly, due to unexpected weaknesses in the material, the split, normally a vertical affair, had turned ninety degrees and now runs parallel to the sole. The split is probably over four inches long.

Now this isn't really a problem. Admittedly if I walk in water more than two inches deep, water comes in. But that's true of pretty well any footwear. Because in summer we don't often get water more than two inches deep, this pair are now summer wellies. As the weather breaks in autumn I'll get a new pair which will be winter wellies, and at some point, hopefully not before late spring, they in their turn will split and become summer wellies.

But by now, my right welly was pretty well full of stinking water and mud. But on the positive side, I'd got the lamb out.
All that was left to do was to carry it home and treat it, because it had now decided that walking is for wimps. Even with Sal's bared teeth inches from its nose it remained obdurate and had to be carried.
Did I say I'd got a busy day planned?
Yeah well, forget that. You've wasted so much time reading this that you've no chance at all of doing the things you intended to do either.

Building communities.

That's what the meeting was about, although that wasn't the title, that's what it did and that was what drove people to attend.
And I drove up from the south, through St John's in the Vale on a gorgeous September morning; the sort that you never get many of. Today the two crags at the sides were bathed in bright sunlight. Blencathra behind was almost lost in a golden haze as the early morning sun burned off the last of the mist. It looked like nothing as much as a Chinese landscape painting.
And later in the day, travelling home, the good folk of the Vale were hard at work. Travelling up I'd seen one field that looked as if it might just bale today, and yes, they were hard at it. A tractor that was older than me pulling a baler which had once had paint on it but was now uniformly rust. New equipment and old, boys barely out of school driving tractors that cost more a month on lease than the monthly rent of a terraced house in Barrow, old men with rakes, cleaning up the corners for the baler.

And in a field that men were mowing before Christianity came to these islands, a young man is loading bales onto a trailer. His surname and his accent are Cumbrian but his eyes are the grey of the waters of the Vistula and at least one of his daughters will have the high cheekbones of his mother and the smile that captured his father's heart. And his grandfather is buried in the churchyard a world away from the Polish home he left to fly a Hurricane.

Communities absorb, they take the good and they make it their own.

And if the world keeps turning and we don't let the political pygmies screw up too badly, in half a century's time a chap in his sixties will turn and say to his son who has eyes as grey as his own, "Stop fretting, we've made good hay in September before."

In some parts of the county we're not building communities, we're trying to make it possible for them to survive, help them negotiate the minefield of tick-boxes and departmental objectives. Someone has to temper the wind to the shorn lamb.

And the communities roll on, season following season, year following year. I saw a chap at a funeral one day and at an agricultural show the next. Our conversation drifted to the funeral and he commented that he's got to the stage when he wonders whether he ought to start leaving a few notes as to what he wants for his funeral.

And he is right. On a wet Mothering Sunday the old lad will go to church with his daughter-in-law because his grandchildren are singing. He's walked from a steading that was old when the Normans finally came to the valley and the church isn't all that much younger. He feels the place in his bones, and when the grandchildren put a posy on his late wife's grave he turns to his daughter and says, "And when my time comes, put me in there with her."

And on a glorious day a month later, when his son takes him up onto the fell on the quad (one of the dogs being forced to run alongside to make room for the old man) and the ewes are looking well and the grass is growing and the lambs are bright, inquisitive and without fear, he breathes deeply and the world he loves floods over him. And when his son stops the quad and they look round, the old man says, "You know, when my time comes, cremate me and have my ashes scattered up here."

And may the Lord have mercy on the clergyman who has to untangle that little lot!

But the cycle continues; the funeral with its grief and shared memories and meeting with old friends on the edge of an open grave. Then there's the baptism, bedlam in a small church, with those who know how to behave in church and those who've never darkened the doorstep before.

And if the vicar knows his job a young couple looking a bit serious because he's explained just what's going on and what they're swearing to do, and asked them whether they really want to make that sort of commitment.

It's funny really, at baptisms and funerals they sit in their cars, or they cluster outside the porch in the drizzle, waiting for enough of them to arrive so they can screw up enough courage to enter the church. A dangerous place where you might have to be silent, or even think.

And the wedding, which shouldn't be sombre but sometimes is as women who were once girls and men who were once lads look down the aisle and the years fall away and they wonder. And the bride, wearing white as she marries the lad she has lived with for three years. But she's right because today is a day where commitment means more than the technicalities of biology and the first time down the aisle is not a road you can walk twice, however often you marry.

And in spite of ourselves, we keep the show on the road somehow, knitting together somehow the threads that make the community and hold it together.

It's wet!

It's been raining.
When I say raining I really mean it's been chucking it down. Even for Cumbria, it's been wet. I was looking sheep this morning. I set off, in full waterproofs and the first job was to collect Sal to take her with me. Normally she's standing outside her kennel full of enthusiasm. Indeed she can leap four feet into the air from a standing start in her delight that we're going to be doing something.
Her kennel by the way is an old cattle trailer. She has a big plastic drum inside that which is really snug and she does sometimes sleep in. But normally she'll sleep under the trailer. And this morning she watched me approach the trailer and crawled out from under it at the last possible moment to join me in our walk through the rain.
And the rain continued to fall. It was so bad I was reminded of that bit from Winnie the Pooh where the rain is so bad the pages of the book start to run!
First down onto the Mosses to check some old ewes with a tup down there, it's wet. All the hollows are full of water, and when Sal wandered off and I called her back to me she took a long and complex path to avoid having to wade to get to me. But the ewes seem to be happy moving about on the drier bits and it's not as if there's a risk of genuine flooding.
Then off to see the others. Walking through one field the path I was walking along was under six inches of water and the water was moving. We've had so much rain that not only is the ground saturated, but it's starting to flow across the surface to run off.
The other ewes weren't too pleased to see me either. I think the endless rain has made them irritable. They moved together into a huddle and glared at me. Every so often one of them would shake herself, pretty much like a dog does. Because of the lanolin in their fleece the water doesn't really soak in to the wool so when a wet sheep shakes herself, you can see the cloud of water thrown off.

And then in for coffee; discard wet clothes and put stuff to dry. It has to be said that there are times when I tell myself that it would be good to get a few cattle again. Build up a small suckler herd, buy some half-bred Hereford heifer calves and rear them, bull them with Angus. Quality meat, easy calving, sell it direct to consumers in freezer packs. It would be more of a hobby than a business to be honest. But it's on days like this, when I think of the work with housed cattle, and the problems of getting slurry out when the ground is waterlogged; I just sigh as I sip my coffee in front of the fire.

Who is this Jim Webster anyway?

Well I've farmed in South Cumbria all my life, milked cows for thirty years, run a suckler herd and reared calves. Now life seems to have afflicted me with sheep.
As well as that I've been a free lance journalist, mainly covering agricultural issues, as well as being the CLA's national livestock adviser for about ten years.
I've also had four fantasy novels published in paperback and innumerable novellas of a similar length to this short collection of stories
To round this off I've got a wife and three daughters, and in spite of this, no dress sense whatsoever.
I've never been able to keep a diary, but over recent years I've written a blog. This is just a collection of blog posts.

Printed in Great Britain
by Amazon